YORK HANDBOOKS

GENERAL EDITOR:
Professor A.N. Jeffares
(*University of Stirling*)

THE
ENGLISH
NOVEL

Ian Milligan

MA M ED (GLASGOW)
Lecturer in English,
University of Stirling

LONGMAN
YORK PRESS

YORK PRESS
Immeuble Esseily, Place Riad Solh, Beirut.

LONGMAN GROUP LIMITED
Longman House,
Burnt Mill,
Harlow,
Essex.

First published 1984
ISBN 0 582 79269 X
Printed in Hong Kong by
Wilture Printing Co Ltd.

Contents

Preface

In this book an attempt has been made to consider the English novel historically, thematically, and technically. Its principal aim, however, is to help readers to become more aware of the variety of the novel as a form of literature, of the pleasure it has to offer, and of the interpretative skills which a careful reading of novels may help to develop. Novelists have many aims: some seek to entertain, some to instruct, some to persuade or even indoctrinate. The best of them, however, have been conscious creators of literary works of art. This book has been written to help readers to develop the critical skills which will enable them to evaluate these intentions for themselves, and to help students to study their chosen field more systematically and effectively.

I am grateful to Professor A. N. Jeffares for encouraging me to write this book. While it was being written, my wife gave me invaluable support, and she has brought to it the careful eye of a devoted teacher. Its faults and limitations are my own.

Department of English Studies   IAN MILLIGAN
The University of Stirling

Chapter 1

Introduction

What is a novel?

Novels are meant to be enjoyed: they can be seen in paperback on every bookstall inviting us to read them, promising pleasure, excitement, escape and adventure among areas of experience hitherto closed to us. They are, if you like, verbal cassettes which can be played on the video-recorder of imagination, stimulating the complicated machinery of fantasy which our brains seem programmed to produce. By looking at a succession of black marks on paper we can be transported to places all over the world; we can share in extraordinary experiences which would not be part of our normal lives; we can meet, understand, and perhaps even sympathise with, saints, criminals, terrorists, political prisoners, policemen – and very ordinary people, whose cramped lives offer little freedom of choice. The conventional definition of a novel tells us that it is a work of fiction, of not less than fifty thousand words, written in prose: but it is also an attempt to convey imaginatively some circumstances significant enough to have an interest for the people who might read it. It is one of the most fluent, diverse and unpredictable of literary forms.

Even if the paragraph you have just read is roughly true, some doubts may have been raised in your mind. Reading a novel is certainly not as automatic as switching on a record-player: the reading of any verbal material is a complex process which demands skills of remembering, interpreting, forecasting, re-ordering and assessing. It does not simply consist of our imaginative response to it: we know what it is like to be caught up in some narrative process which is 'unreal' – whether it is reading a book, or watching a film or television serial; but however deeply involved we become in this process, we cannot just let our imagination run freely. If we do, we soon discover that we are missing too much of the story. When we listen to music, which has a narrative to be followed, even if it might be impossible to put it into words, it is easy for us to stop following the music and to be distracted by the irrelevant, unstable contents of our own minds. Instead of understanding what is being said, we are drifting in a world of our own, out of contact, 'day-dreaming': instead of practising the skill of disciplined, imaginative attention, we have given ourselves up to fantasy.

What is a novel, then? Is it the printed contents of this volume I hold in my hands, or is it a transaction which takes place between the reader and the book? Perhaps the same question might be asked of the performance of a piece of music, or of a play. Each of these seems more obviously 'open' and incomplete as it lies on the printed page, requiring the effort of a great many people – instrumentalists or actors, stage designers, producers or conductors – to bring it to life. A novel may seem less open to interpretation, rather more a question of correctly interpreting the written intentions of the author. But closer reflection may prompt us to wonder whether this is so.

Certainly, the private, apparently passive, activity of reading a novel may take a number of forms. It can be strenuous, exacting, challenging, testing, or it can be easy, automatic, routine. Any kind of reading involves the exercise of a skill which most of us have been learning for a very long time. As with any skill, we can stay within the limits of what we have already learnt or we can make deliberate efforts to extend the scope of our ability. Reading is often taken to mean the exercise of already practised skills in a routine way. If we hear a friend say, 'It's raining tonight: I'm going to stay at home and read a good book', we probably assume that he (or she) is going to make himself comfortable, that he will find something by an author he knows and likes, or that he will get out something he has read before. It is not, we gather, an evening for the strenuous or the adventurous. Nothing wrong with that, of course. There is a time for performing the old strokes, and rehearsing well-practised routines: it comforts, consoles and reassures us. There is a special pleasure in doing what we know we can do well: why go out of our depth? Indeed, novels have often been written to provide a means of entertainment or a vehicle for escape from the boring and the humdrum.

Adding to our repertoire of skills is an often painful but, surely, invariably rewarding experience. But, the reader might well ask, what skills are involved in reading a novel? A major one is the extension of our power of interpreting language. If we read widely among novels in English, we shall encounter the most extraordinary range of ways of processing the language. We shall be able to experience its development through time and be aware of its divergences in the dialects and regional variations which have occurred because of the dispersion of English throughout the world. These encounters with the infinite variety of linguistic styles are not, of course, peculiar to the novel; they can equally be found in poetry, drama and the literature of non-fictional prose. But reading a novel presents special problems to the reader because the novel has traditionally attempted to offer an experience of life, or reality, through narrative, commentary and the interaction of characters, particularly through dialogue. The novelist appears to make a claim that what he is telling us is in some sense true. The novel has been used to report on people and places, to introduce readers to new environments and conditions of life; it has been used to make an interpretation or assessment of contemporary ways of life and the manners and customs of currently dominant social classes; it has been used to create new modes of feeling, new fashions, new interests and tastes; it has been used to offer symbolic accounts of the destiny of mankind and affirmations of what are the most significant experiences and most laudable pursuits in human life. Novels have made the most minutely particular assertions about how things are, and have given the most grandly prophetic accounts of how things might be. The words of the novelist have power to move us to action, or to elate or depress us: it is of considerable consequence to the reader that he should be able to withstand their effect. The world of the novel is a new creation, imaginatively conceived, which may be governed by laws quite different from our own.

To enter the imaginary world of the novelist requires a co-operative effort on the part of the reader. It is in the reader's understanding that the strange transformation takes place of word and sentence and paragraph into place and character, action and event. Just as writers sometimes talk about being 'taken over' by the characters they have invented, so readers know what it is like to 'believe' in fictional characters and places. At their most powerful, such attitudes may easily result in the public expression of grief when fictional characters die, or in the gifts which are sent to them on their purely imaginary birthdays or wedding anniversaries. Characters in series or serials, in books or on television and radio, seem specially likely to generate these attachments. Dickens's Little Nell (in his *The Old Curiosity Shop*, 1841), and the BBC's Doris Archer appeared regularly in printed or broadcast form from some place of publication which seemed to locate them in a physical space where they might live beyond the bounds of the monthly number or the daily broadcast.

Characters who exist only within the covers of the book we hold in our own hands may take a less powerful hold on the imagination. But characters such as Sir Arthur Conan Doyle's Sherlock Holmes, Dickens's Mr Pickwick or Ian Fleming's James Bond have taken on a life of their own, exhibiting a vitality which has apparently made them independent of their original context. If they are killed off, like Sherlock Holmes, their return is demanded by readers. When their creator dies, as Ian Fleming did in mid-career, other writers are prevailed upon to prolong their lives in new adventures. They easily survive transplantation from one medium to another – from book to stage or to film. Places, too, can emerge from a succession of novels with a detailed density of field and hedgerow, house and landscape which prompts readers to produce maps of the Barsetshire of Anthony Trollope (1815–82) or the Wessex of Thomas Hardy (1840–1928), of the Middle Earth of J. R. R. Tolkien (1892–1972) or the Yoknapatawpha County of William

Faulkner (1897–1962). All this is evidence enough of the willingness of readers to enter into the fictions which have been produced for them and to co-operate with authors in the making of places real enough to accommodate the characters they have come to know as well as their own friends and neighbours.

What is the nature of this co-operative action between reader and writer? Some of it arises from the fact that readers must usually go beyond the information they are given by the writer. A novel is necessarily selective: there is a limit to the information we can be given about persons, places and events. Modern psychology has suggested that much complex human behaviour depends upon the interpretation of fragmentary impressions. Out of the minimal information which a glance or a touch may give us, we make inferences and come to conclusions about total situations which are much too complex for us to know in detail. Human interaction depends upon the rapid assessment we make of the hints which experience gives us. Again and again, we reach conclusions which are only partly supported by the evidence before us. Memory helps us here: new problems are solved because we categorise them in the light of situations we have dealt with in the past. There are habits, conventions and codes which help us to identify and classify the people, places and situations which we have to deal with. Clothes, speech-habits, attitudes and manners can be used to label people, positively or negatively.

In reading a novel, we make use of all these human capacities for dealing with information. We readily apply the metaphors and symbols, which allow us to see one term or set of terms in the light of, and by analogy with, some quite different and unrelated term or set of terms. From the parts and fragments which the writer offers us, we are able to construct a whole; in the current of words and phrases, which we read, we begin to discern patterns which have a coherent design. Novelists make use of established social codes, so that the conventions of the everyday world mould the characters and mark the behaviour of the fictional world. But the novel is not simply a mirror of society: if that were so, the only work for the reader would be that of recognition, and the mark of the successful novelist would be how well he had reduplicated in his fiction the conventions of 'real life'. Part of the task of the novelist throughout history has been to bring home to readers the artificiality of the conventions by which they live. A rigidly controlled society may succeed in suppressing the tension between social conventions and the desire for change which arises spontaneously in its members; but the novel has flourished most when writers have been free to explore the contradictions and confusions which arise when the behaviour a society prescribes is out of step with what its people want to do.

It may well be that the appeal which the novel has for readers is connected to the freedom which it gives them to work with the novelist in constructing a version of reality. One of the conventions of the classical novel of the eighteenth and nineteenth centuries was that the novelist appeared in person to conduct a dialogue with the reader: he appealed to the reader for support, or approval, he invited him to make his own judgments of the action and events which lay between reader and writer like a battleground or chess-board or football-field upon which complicated games might be played with their own rules and strategies. As the writer in one of his roles made the game happen, so in another he commented upon what was happening or engaged in a discussion with the reader about the action that was taking place. Such a method of story-telling might, of course, simply be a pretence on the part of the author, if he used the story merely as a vehicle for his own opinions. He could not win the interest of the reader, if he left him no real freedom to make up his own mind about the action and events of which the story was composed. Equally, the reader's interest would be limited if the action were too predictable, or if the characters and their behaviour offered him no challenge.

To the reading of a novel, the reader brings a knowledge of the habits, customs and codes of his own society as well as a tolerant acquaintance with the rich possibilities of human character and behaviour, and the impulses, desires and affections which form and motivate them. But as he reads the novel itself, following its sentences and paragraphs and chapters, knowledge and expectations, peculiar to the novel itself, begin to form in his mind. His memory of what has happened causes him to form predictions about how things will go. The actions of the fictitious characters establish new norms of behaviour which might conform to, or contrast with, the codes of his own society. The action of the novel has a pattern of its own which he might be invited to sympathise with or to criticise. The measure of the novelist's success lies in how far he arouses the interest and attention of the reader, to what extent he enlists his active participation in making the novel and how skilful he is in creating characters and devising situations which might surprise or disconcert or puzzle the reader so that he is compelled to find justification for the actions of the characters.

The first great European novel of modern times, from which all others may be said to have sprung – *Don Quixote* (1605, 1615) by Miguel de Cervantes Saavedra (1547–1616) – takes as its subject the clash between the conventional expectations of its hero, Don Quixote, and his unexpected encounters with everyday life in seventeenth-century Spain. But it also raises the central literary question of what happens when a writer tries to describe experience in words: what can a writer do, when his attempts to describe, or imitate, falsify and distort the limitless stream of sensations which human conventions try vainly to restrain. Only the writer knows how inadequate his words are to capture the elusive sense of what it is to be alive; only the writer knows how easy it is to charm and hypnotise his readers into accepting that his flow of language corresponds to the truth of things; only the writer knows in how many different ways a situation or state of affairs might be represented; only the writer knows how much he needs the reader to give organised and substantial life to the sentences he has written, by making links, drawing conclusions, inferring, deducing, seeing patterns, establishing relationships and bridging gaps between what is stated and what is suggested and implied, between what is actual, what is possible, and what is consistent with some broader explanation or design than any that is explicitly given in the novel itself.

Studying the novel

The argument so far implies that the novel needs attentive readers. It also suggests that the variety of novels is so great that it may be difficult to find general rules which will apply to all novels. Individual novels need to be read according to the rules and conventions which the writer has established for that particular book. Any generalisation about the novel can only come from a wide acquaintanceship with many texts. The purpose of this Handbook is to attempt to offer a framework within which the reading of individual novels may be organised, so that the reader may gradually form a picture of the nature and development of this kind of literature, and be able to judge what methods of reading may best be applied to the novels he may choose (or be required) to read.

Part of the problem of becoming acquainted with the novel is that its roots go deep into the history of literature. The novel may seem the most modern of literary kinds, but it is linked historically with other forms of literature, such as the epic and the drama, which reach back to the beginnings of the literary consciousness of the Western world. Chapter 2 of this Handbook isolates for special study four types of the novel form which appeared early in its modern history and which have appeared singly and in combination during its subsequent development. Any sharp separation of such basic types or patterns is bound to be rather artificial but this approach will emphasise from the beginning that the object of our study is the nature of the form of the novel.

Although the novel as we know it today has drawn its material and its methods of story-telling from many sources, its modern origin may be traced to the work of the seventeenth-century Spanish writer Cervantes, who wrote a fiction in prose partly as a parody of the impossible adventures and extravagant manners depicted in the romances which were the dominant literary form at that time. *Don Quixote* modified what was then accepted as the established conventions of imaginative fiction. Cervantes challenged these conventions by an appeal to the probable and the real. Romance idealised human beings so that the behaviour of its readers might be improved: it depicted heroic encounters between the impossibly good and the incorrigibly evil. By parodying these exploits in his account of the adventures of Don Quixote, Cervantes did not mean to disparage the virtues praised by writers of romance: he wished to explore the feasibility of their realisation by imperfect human beings. Whereas the verse and prose romances of earlier writers had been inspired by visionary glimpses of a human nature set free from its limitations, Cervantes wished to describe the endless conflict which exists between what men aspire to and what they can perform. In Don Quixote and Sancho Panza he devised apt and vivid means of giving individual character to these abstract conceptions: knight and peasant signify the uneasy union between body and spirit; the peasant's struggle to keep alive only appears to be at odds with the knight's imaginative freedom and independence of mind. In reality they are inseparable. By taking as his subject-matter the practical consequences of human action, Cervantes mapped out part of the territory of the modern novel; by his awareness of the puzzling nature of fiction itself and its teasing relationship to the real he pointed the way for later writers who wished to explore beyond the frontiers of the realistic novel.

The novel emerged once more in England at the beginning of the eighteenth century in the form of a fictional imitation of the diaries, autobiographies, travellers' tales and biographies of criminals which were common forms of prose literature in earlier years. Daniel Defoe (?1661–1731), after an adventurous life working as a spy in government service, began writing, when he was nearly sixty, books which were different from the many pamphlets and tracts on political, economic, social and religious problems which he had produced during a long and prolific career. These works of imagination were attempts to enter into the lives and characters of thieves, highwaymen, prostitutes and sailor-and-soldier adventurers. Defoe was ambivalent about the nature of these fictions. He was keen to insist on their truthfulness and on his own role as a clerk or amanuensis, who put the stories in words suitable for publication. As he put it in the preface to *Moll Flanders* (1721–2):

> The author is here supposed to be writing her own history, and in the very beginning of her account she gives the reasons why she thinks fit to conceal her true name, after which there is no occasion to say any more about that.
> It is true that the original of this story is put into new words, and the style of the famous lady we here speak of is a little altered; particularly

she is made to tell her own tale in modester words than she told it at first, the copy which came first to hand having been written in language more like one still in Newgate* than one grown penitent and humble, as she afterwards pretends to be.

The pen employed in finishing her story, and making it what you now see it to be, has had no little difficulty to put it into a dress fit to be seen, and to make it speak a language fit to be read.

Even today among religious or other groups whose aim is to change lives, the value of the testimony of penitents is not forgotten. Sinners, alcoholics or the overweight are encouraged to explain how they came to abandon their wicked ways so that others may profit from their example. Essentially, Defoe's fictions aimed to edify and improve those who read them. As author, he claimed to be merely the ventriloquist who spoke for the penitent: his success lay in devising a style of presentation of such authenticity and naturalness that it might well be taken to be true.

But the development of the novel is a European phenomenon of considerable complexity. Among the immediate predecessors of Cervantes's novel in Spanish literature were short tales about rogues and rascals who devote their energies to getting back at a world which they think has treated them harshly. The Spanish word *picaro*, or good-for-nothing, gave the name 'picaresque' to novels of this kind. They are down-to-earth and 'realistic' in the sense that they take a pessimistic view of the possibility of human goodness; their view of life is mean and harsh and cynical. One of the earliest of these novels is the anonymously written *Lazarillo de Tormes* (1554), which was followed by *Guzmán de Alfarache* (1599–1604) by Mateo Alemán (?1547–1614). Some aspects of this Spanish tradition came through France – especially through the novel *Gil Blas* (1715–35)) by Alain-René Le Sage (1668–1747) – to Tobias Smollett (1721–71), a Scot, whose *Roderick Random* (1748) and *Peregrine Pickle* (1751) had some of the features associated with this kind of novel, although their principal characters were certainly not portrayed as rogues.

A quite different kind of fiction was initiated by an English printer, Samuel Richardson (1689–1761), whose first novel, *Pamela*, appeared in 1740. This novel took the form of a series of letters exchanged mainly between the heroine, Pamela, and her parents. The technique of Richardson's fiction was strikingly new: characters and situations were presented with an immediacy which earlier writers of fiction had not attempted; there was a much more poignant sense of the feelings of the characters; and the moral climate of Richardson's novel was entirely different from the ruthless cynicism of the picaresque novel.

*Newgate: the name of the prison which for centuries served the City of London and the County of Middlesex.

It was left to Henry Fielding (1707–54), while reacting against what he thought was the hypocrisy and sentimentality of Richardson, to link this new form of English literature with Cervantes and the mainstream of the classical tradition. In *Joseph Andrews* (1742) and *Tom Jones* (1749) he invented what he called 'the comic epic in prose', establishing the narrator as a principal figure in the narrative and conferring on his new form a weight, dignity and breadth of human interest which could bear comparison with any other form of literature which preceded it. Later in the century, Laurence Sterne (1713–68), the fourth founding father of the English novel, wrote the first 'experimental novel' to demonstrate that a form which had been invented could as easily be disassembled, and that there was nothing sacrosanct about its conventions. In *Tristram Shandy* (1760–67) he produced a novel which, in contrast to the works of Defoe, constantly reminded the reader that it was a fiction.

This preliminary sketch of how the English novel began has shown how diverse its antecedents were. The simplest approach to any example of the form shows how much there is to observe. The subject matter of the story, the language in which it is told, the customs, assumptions and ways of behaving which it brings to our attention, and the methods by which it assembles its material, provide a seemingly endless array of material for study. To begin at the beginning and to move through the history of the form might seem an impossibly burdensome task.

A thematic approach

One way of reducing the density of material which is offered by the novel in English from the eighteenth to the twentieth century is to adopt a thematic approach to its study. The student's first aim should be to find some method of making a selection from the available material and of grouping it under manageable headings which will allow for easier assimilation and for cross-references to be made between the selected items. Groups of novels which have been selected according to their main topic or theme can be formed without reference to divisions of time or geography, although some groupings will arise naturally from some common regional or historical link. Within the history of the novel, recurrent topics have been treated by generations of novelists; by studying such themes through history, the student may become more aware of the qualities which novels written in different periods and cultures may nevertheless have in common. A comparison of the contemporary with the historically remote may reveal human patterns of behaviour which endure through time, and it may help to make what may initially seem alien and unsympathetic more acceptable to current taste. Chapter 3 of this Handbook will look in closer detail at themes which have persisted through the history of the novel.

A formal approach

Yet another way of studying the novel is to pay attention to its formal elements. A modern critic, Wolfgang Iser, has described the novel as 'a system of perspectives designed to transmit the individuality of the author's vision [of the world]'. He believes that reading a novel requires a high degree of active participation from the reader, who must recognise and synthesise the perspectives which the author has written into the text of the novel. It is the reader's act of synthesis or interpretation, in Iser's view, which creates the text. Among the perspectives which offer guidelines to the interpreter are those established by the narrator, the characters, the plot, and a further perspective which Iser calls 'the fictitious reader'. By this term, he means the implicit or intended reader whom the author had in mind when he wrote the novel. This perspective will be closest to the assumptions of the audience which was contemporary with the writer. Readers of nineteenth-century novels will be aware that the author frequently addresses his readers, sometimes inviting their agreement, sometimes challenging their assumptions. The modern reader cannot identify with this 'implied reader' but he must acknowledge that this perspective – the perspective of the author's contemporaries – is a recognisable strand in the structure of the text.

Iser describes the reader's task in the following way:

> As a rule there are four main perspectives [in the novel]: those of the narrator, the characters, the plot and the fictitious reader. Although these may differ in order of importance, none of them on its own is identical to the meaning of the text. What they do is to provide guidelines originating from different starting points (narrator, characters etc.), continually shading into each other and devised in such a way that they all converge on a general meeting place. We call this meeting place the meaning of the text, which can only be brought into focus if it is visualized from a standpoint. Thus, standpoint and convergence of textual perspectives are closely interrelated, although neither of them is actually represented in the text, let alone set out in words.*

No text, according to Iser, wears its meaning on its sleeve. The novel contains its meaning, but does not utter it. There is no passage in it which says, 'this is what this novel means'. If any novel did something like this, it would hold little interest for the reader, since putting meanings together is what readers enjoy doing. Recognising the principal strands of meaning in the novel and judging their relationships are the special business of the reader; only he can bring them into

*Wolfgang Iser, *The Act of Reading*, Routledge and Kegan Paul, London, 1978, p. 35.

coherence and establish a satisfactory meaning for the novel as a whole. In Iser's view, it follows that no one final, or 'correct', meaning can be established for the novel. Each reader of the text will bring something from his own experience which will show the text in a different light and add to the richness of its meanings. It is this feature of the inexhaustibility of the text which gives reading its fascination.

If there is truth in this attractive view of 'the necessary reader', it suggests that one valuable way of studying the novel is to be as clear as we can about the elements of the novel which carry its meanings. How can the reader in any individual instance bring the novel's perspectives into focus and find the standpoint from which they make the most coherent sense? Chapter 4 of this Handbook looks more closely at the structure of the novel.

The historical approach

To build up a sense of the historical development of the novel is a legitimate and desirable aim for the student. At an elementary stage of our study, there may be some point in disregarding the differences of history which distinguish one work from another. At a later stage, it is satisfying to have some grasp of the changes which time has produced within any form of art. We can then see how themes and techniques have been developed by a succession of writers who are aware of their relationships to each other. Gradually, the student will acquire a sense of the tradition of the form in which he is interested. This awareness demands time and effort; there is no short-cut to it by means of summary or digest. Knowledge about works of art can never take the place of direct acquaintance with them. Slowly and patiently, we must build up our own direct personal knowledge of the novel by coming to know individual works and the work of individual novelists. Gradually, we may come to see broader rhythms of change and development which have taken place over the centuries. Some rough framework may be useful for this purpose, however, and a straightforward chronological table may serve as a map with which to explore in detail the tracks which writers have made in the course of developing the novel. Such an outline map will be found on pp. 114–21 of this Handbook.

Using the Handbook

While the Handbook can give general hints and suggestions for approaching the study of the novel, the student's knowledge of the novel depends upon his understanding of individual texts. Reference will be made to a considerable number of novels, many of which are the subject of separate treatment in books in the companion series, *York Notes*. A satisfactory understanding of the novel can only come about through a close study of the language of the novel, and the Handbook contains many extracts from the text of novels, with detailed comments. Possibly the best way to use this Handbook is to read it through carefully and to apply to one of the sections in Chapter 3 ('Themes') the methods of study which have been set out in Chapter 4 ('Technique'). Chapter 2 is an essential preparation for Chapter 4, but it also lays the foundation for the historical approach to the study of the novel.

Chapter 2

Types

Introduction

Before we begin to examine the types and themes of the novel, which are our concern in Chapters 2 and 3, we must enter a note of caution. For the last two centuries the idea of literary genres, or 'kinds', has not been welcome to writers or critics. In earlier centuries critics who believed in such divisions stressed the notion of rules to which writers had to conform, if they wanted their works to be successful. But since the beginning of the Romantic movement at the end of the eighteenth century, art has tried to break down the barriers between its different means of expression. The novel itself has resisted classification. Each novelist, it might be said, creates his own kind of novel; we think of 'the Dickensian novel', or 'the novel of William Faulkner' meaning by these terms novels which are a characteristic product of their authors. We are accustomed to speak of the novelist's 'world', as if in creating his fictions, he has struck out from the unformalised chaos of ideas, possible forms of conduct and ways of seeing the world, a new territory which he has made substantial and habitable. As the French critic Tzvetan Todorov has put it, 'As a rule, the literary masterpiece does not enter into any genre save perhaps its own'.*

In a later chapter we shall consider what characteristics give novels their sense of individual identity. In this chapter we shall be concerned with a small number of novels, written near the beginning of the history of the form in England, which may be regarded as fundamental types – as the basic genetic material from which later novels have been derived. Fictions which resemble novels had been written at many times and in many places throughout history – in ancient Egypt, in Greece, in Rome and in Japan. The *Satyricon* (*c.*AD50) by Petronius (*d.*AD66), *The Golden Ass* (*c.*AD150) by Lucius Apuleius (*b.*AD125), *Daphnis and Chloe* (*c.*AD200) by Longus (3rd c. AD) and the Japanese *The Tale of Genji* (*c.*1020) by Lady Murasaki (?978–?1031) can still be read with great pleasure by modern readers. But it was not until a number of fictional forms fused together in eighteenth-century Europe that the form we now recognise achieved a settled identity.

*Tzvetan Todorov, *The Poetics of Prose*, Basil Blackwell, Oxford, 1977, p. 43.

The picaresque novel

We have already referred to the influence which the sixteenth-century Spanish novel dealing with the lives of thieves and vagabonds came to have on the European novel. The first of these novels was the anonymously written *Lazarillo de Tormes* (1554). This short, lively book traces the career of the son of a servant-girl from his first employment as the guide of a blind man to his ultimate attainment of social responsibility, when he becomes a member of the Civil Service – the town-crier, in fact. Lazaro's masters – priest, poor gentleman, pardoner and constable – are described in a series of sketches which throw a satirical light on the social conditions of the day. The life of the *picaro* is portrayed as precarious, violent, deceitful and insecure. Goaded by hunger to live by his wits, Lazaro is glad to attain a measure of stability. As he tells us towards the end of his tale,

> I was a well set-up young man by now and one day, when I was in the cathedral, one of the priests gave me a job. He provided me with a donkey, four jugs and a whip and I began to carry water around the city. That was my first step towards becoming a respectable citizen because my hunger was satisfied.

Something of Lazaro's self-protective resourcefulness can still be seen in Charles Dickens's Sam Weller (in *The Pickwick Papers*, 1836). Alain-René Le Sage, a Breton writer who had never been to Spain, adapted the tradition of the picaresque novel in *The Adventures of Gil Blas of Santillane* which was published in four volumes between 1715 and 1735. This is a much more ambitious narrative. Gil Blas is a respectable young man who is sent off by his uncle to study at the University of Salamanca. Although he falls among thieves, he is not a thief himself; his adventures take him through every section of society from the dishonest and rascally to the court of the prince; his own story serves as a frame for the life histories of many of the men and women he meets on his travels. What is most striking about Le Sage's novel is its wealth of incidents. In his essay on 'The Art of Fiction' (1888) Henry James (1843–1916) made the famous remark, 'What is character but the determination of incident? What is incident but the illustration of character?' In other words, what a man is results in actions of a certain kind; what he does shows us what kind of man he is. But this assumption scarcely applies to the picaresque novel which is rather a record of events than of actions. Here, from Chapter Eleven of the First Book, is the history of a lady whom Gil Blas has been forced to take prisoner by the group of robbers into whose hands he had himself fallen at the beginning of his journey:

> I was born at Valladolid, and am called Donna Mencia de Mosquera. My father, Don Martin, after spending most of his family estate in the

service, was killed in Portugal at the head of his regiment. He left me so little property that I was a bad match, though an only daughter. I was not, however, without my admirers, notwithstanding the mediocrity of my fortune. Several of the most considerable cavaliers in Spain sought me in marriage. My favourite was Don Alvar de Mello. It is true he had a prettier person than his rivals; but more solid qualities determined me in his favour. He had wit, discretion, valour, probity; and in addition to all these, an air of fashion. Was an entertainment to be given? His taste was sure to be displayed. If he appeared in the lists, he always fixed the eyes of the beholders on his strength and dexterity. I singled him out from all the rest, and married him.

A few days after our nuptials, he met Don Andrew de Baesa, who had been his rival, in a private place. They attacked one another sword in hand, and Don Andrew fell. As he was nephew to the corregidor* of Valladolid, a turbulent man, violently incensed against the house of Mello, Don Alvar thought he could not soon enough make his escape. He returned home speedily, and told what had happened while his horse was getting ready. My dear Mencia, said he at length, we must part. You know the corregidor: let us not flatter ourselves; he will hunt us even to death. You are unacquainted with his influence; this empire will be too hot to hold me. He was so penetrated by his own grief and mine as not to be able to articulate further. I made him take some cash and jewels: then he folded me in his arms, and we did nothing but mingle our sighs and tears for a quarter of an hour. In a short time the horse was at the door. He tore himself from me, and left me in a condition not easily expressed.

This tiny fragment of the twelve books of *Gil Blas* gives a not unfair impression of the whole. It is characterised by a dense rapidity of action which throws little light on the nature of the events or on the character of the participants. There is a strange discrepancy between the impressive names of the characters and their lack of personality. Above all, the reader is not allowed to come close to the action which the narrative describes; it is the general features, not the details of the story with which the narrator is concerned. As we might expect, Gil Blas is a far stronger character, who tells his own tale with much liveliness. But he too is largely concerned with the external events he describes; the reader is not taken into his confidence or allowed to share his deepest feelings. Here is Gil in the hands of justice:

The corregidor, whose office was suspicion, set me down for the culprit; and presuming on the lady for an accomplice, ordered us into separate custody. This magistrate was none of your stern gallows-

*corregidor: the chief magistrate of a Spanish town.

preaching fellows, he had a jocular epigrammatic sort of countenance.
God knows if his heart lay in the right place for all that! As soon as I
was committed, in came he with his pack. They knew their trade, and
began by searching me. What a forfeit to these lords of the manor! At
every handful of pistoles,* what little eyes did I see them make! The
corregidor was absolutely out of his wits! It was the best stroke within
the memory of justice! My pretty lad, said his Worship with a softened
tone, we only do our duty, but do not tremble for your bones before
the time: you will not be broken on the wheel if you do not deserve it.
These blood-suckers were emptying my pockets all the time with their
cursed palaver, and took from me . . . my uncle's forty ducats. They
stuck at nothing! Their staunch fingers, with slow but certain scent,
routed me out from top to toe; they whisked me round and round, and
stripped me even to the shame of modesty, for fear some sneaking
portrait of the king should slink between my shirt and skin. When
they could sift me no further, the corregidor thought it time to begin
his examination. I told a plain tale. My deposition was taken down;
and the sequel was, that he carried in his train his bloodhounds and
my little property, leaving me to toss without a rag upon a beggarly
wisp of straw.

A combination of two factors holds the reader's attention here – a
simple appetite for knowing what comes next, and a more sophisticated
taste for the flavour of the language of the novel. This presents Gil as the
helpless victim of a set of rogues, superintended by the chief justice, who
search him minutely for any money he may have, so that they can filch it
from him. The idea of Justice, severe and impartial, concerned only for
what is good, is travestied by this 'pack' of 'blood-suckers' who make
'little eyes' at one another when they see Gil's gold. Their fingers are
described metaphorically as a pack of game-dogs on the scent for
money, devotedly snuffling around Gil to see what they can find. As a
'forfeit', he has lost all the rights of the innocent. 'It was the best stroke
within the memory of justice' suggests that the corregidor's men behave
exactly like a band of robbers lying in wait for whatever rich prize may
come their way.

The above passage is based on the translation of the novel made by
Tobias Smollett in 1749, the year after he had published his own novel,
Roderick Random. In the preface to his novel, Smollett pays tribute to
Cervantes and Le Sage, who had 'reformed the taste of mankind' by
directing fiction away from the improbable romances of the Middle
Ages and using it instead to 'point out the follies of ordinary life'.
Smollett admits that he has used *Gil Blas* as a model but claims that he
has kept closer to reality. Here is how he describes his intention:

*pistoles: Spanish gold coins.

I have attempted to represent modest merit struggling with every difficulty to which a friendless orphan is exposed, from his own want of experience, as well as from the selfishness, envy, malice, and base indifference of mankind. To secure a favourable prepossession, I have allowed him the advantage of birth and education, which, in the series of his misfortunes, will, I hope, engage the ingenuous more warmly in his behalf; and though I foresee that some people will be offended at the mean scenes in which he is involved, I persuade myself the judicious will not only perceive the necessity of describing those situations, to which he must of course be confined, in his low state, but also find entertainment in viewing those parts of life, where the humours and passions are undisguised by affectation, ceremony or education; and the whimsical peculiarities of disposition appear as nature has implanted them.

Here Smollett is appealing to a much wider range of interests than Le Sage did. He expects the reader to be sympathetic rather than merely curious, but open-minded enough to look dispassionately on the raw scenes of low life in which his chosen form of the picaresque novel compels him to place his hero. Random, his hero's surname, hints at the chances to which he will be subject, but Smollett has taken a decisive step away from his Spanish and French models by making him a man of good birth. The circumstances in which Roderick finds himself are due to the ill-will of his grandfather as much as to chance. Like Tom Jones, the hero of Fielding's novel of that name (1749), and like Dickens's Oliver Twist, Roderick is saved from his surroundings by his innate good breeding. Even if Roderick Random is no rascal, Smollett keeps him moving. Press-ganged in London, he sails to the West Indies; on his return to England, he is kidnapped and taken to France by smugglers in the pay of a jealous rival for the beautiful Narcissa, the niece of a poetess, to whom Roderick has been recommended by someone who passes for the village witch. Smollett's 'realism' finds expression in the sordid details of eighteenth-century life – the blowing-out of brains, hacking-off of limbs and the emptying of chamber-pots – rather than in the plausibility of his plot.

After Smollett the picaresque novel moved in two directions. One leads through Captain Marryat (1792–1848), excellent writer of such stories of the sea as *Peter Simple* (1834) and *Mr Midshipman Easy* (1836), to the long line of episodic adventure stories, written 'for boys of all ages' by such writers as G. A. Henty (1832–1902), Robert Louis Stevenson (1850–94), H. Rider Haggard (1856–1925), Sir Arthur Quiller-Couch (1863–1944) and John Masefield (1878–1967). The other development of the picaresque novel leads to Charles Dickens (1812–70), in whose hands its potentialities were transformed.

In *David Copperfield* (1850) Dickens has given us an account of David's boyhood reading which is largely autobiographical. It is worth quoting in full because it·suggests not only the tradition on which Dickens drew, but also the power of books on the imagination of the young. David Copperfield describes here how he found comfort in them during the grim period of his life when he took lessons in Latin grammar under the strict supervision of his stepfather and Miss Murdstone:

My father had left a small collection of books in a little room up-stairs to which I had access (for it adjoined my own) and which nobody else in our house ever troubled. From that blessed little room, Roderick Random, Peregrine Pickle, Humphrey Clinker, Tom Jones, the Vicar of Wakefield, Don Quixote, Gil Blas and Robinson Crusoe, came out, a glorious host, to keep me company. They kept alive my fancy . . . – they, and the Arabian Nights, and the Tales of the Genii – and did me no harm; for whatever harm was in some of them was not there for me; *I* knew nothing of it. It is astonishing to me now, how I found time in the midst of my porings and blunderings over heavier themes, to read those books as I did. It is curious to me how I could ever have consoled myself under my small troubles (which were great troubles to me), by impersonating my favourite characters in them – as I did – and by putting Mr. and Miss Murdstone into all the bad ones – which I did too. I have been Tom Jones (a child's Tom Jones, a harmless creature) for a week together. I have sustained my own idea of Roderick Random for a month at a stretch, I verily believe. I had a greedy relish for a few volumes of Voyages and Travels – I forget what, now – that were on those shelves; and for days and days I can remember to have gone about my region of our house, armed with the centre-piece out of an old set of boot-trees – the perfect realisation of Captain Somebody, of the Royal British Navy, in danger of being beset by savages, and resolved to sell his life at a great price. The Captain never lost dignity, from having his ears boxed with the Latin Grammar. I did; but the Captain was a Captain and a hero, in despite of all the grammars of all the languages in the world, dead or alive.

That passage not only tells us something about the English novel, it clarifies some of the changes that took place in it between the eighteenth and the nineteenth centuries. As compared with its eighteenth-century predecessors (however much David admired them), *David Copperfield* is very different in tone. Dickens is careful to dissociate young David from the grosser aspects of the novels he mentions. His prose conveys a reflective inwardness which is very different from Smollett's directness and comparative crudity. Between *Roderick Random* and *David Copperfield* lies a radical shift in the sensibility of the novel-reading public: Roderick Random is tough, unsentimental, uninhibited; David Copperfield is divided, anxious and guilty, one of the first of a long line of modern heroes, damaged by a repressive upbringing, sensitive, timorous, with a longing for ideal relationships which are never likely to be realised. Whereas Smollett looks on human behaviour with the detachment of a surgeon and the black humour of a cantankerous man, Dickens is gentle, vulnerable, reflective, more drawn to the ideal world of fantasy than to the realm of disagreeable fact.

Dickens's early novels from *The Pickwick Papers* (1836) to *Martin Chuzzlewit* (1844) owe much to the picaresque tradition. Consider *The Pickwick Papers* in which Mr Pickwick and three other members of the Pickwick Club, Winkle, the sportsman, Snodgrass, the poet, and Tupman, the lover, set out on their adventures so that they may send 'from time to time, authenticated accounts of their journeys and investigations, of their observations of characters and manners, and of the whole of their adventures, together with all tales and papers to which local scenery or associations may give rise' (*The Pickwick Papers*, Chapter 1). There is nothing of the *picaro* about Mr Pickwick and his friends, but Dickens draws on his boyhood reading of the picaresque novels to construct his tale of the adventures of the Pickwickians. During the course of the novel they complete five tours; the first takes them south-east from London to Rochester where they meet their fellow club-member, Mr Wardle, who takes them to the Manor Farm at Dingley Dell. There Alfred Jingle, a strolling player who foists himself on their company, elopes to London with Mr Wardle's unmarried, middle-aged sister. In the second, they travel from London to Suffolk where they are present at the farcical demagoguery of the Eatanswill election and are invited to the fancy-dress garden party of Mrs Leo Hunter, poetess. During their adventures, Mr Jingle and his lugubrious man-servant, Job Trotter, have a habit of turning up on some nefarious enterprise usually connected with marriageable women of private means. A third journey finds them in Ipswich where Mr Jingle is paying court to the daughter of the local magistrate. After a Christmas excursion to Dingley Dell, Mr Pickwick stands trial in London in an action for breach of promise of marriage brought against him by his landlady. After the verdict against him is brought in, he sets off on a trip to Bath, where he enjoys the idle pleasures of the Assembly Rooms before returning to London to serve a sentence in the Fleet prison, because he refuses to pay costs awarded to his landlady's lawyers, Dodson and Fogg. His final journey takes him to Bristol, then to Birmingham, to sort out the affairs of Mr Winkle and Miss Arabella Allen, who have married without the consent of Mr Winkle's father or of Miss Allen's brother, who had intended her for his best friend, Bob Sawyer. After some vicissitudes all ends happily: Mr Winkle and

Arabella Allen marry, Mr Snodgrass marries Emily Wardle, and Sam Weller, Mr Pickwick's servant, marries his sweetheart, Mary.

Like *Roderick Random, The Pickwick Papers* has a plot which, when summarised, tells us little about the significance of the novel. Compared with its substance, the novel's formal structure is merely the machinery by which Mr Pickwick and his friends are moved from place to place. The substance of the novel is a movement of the imagination which is only indirectly connected to the journeys of the Pickwick Club. In spirit *The Pickwick Papers* moves from the innocent days of the founding of the Club through the darkness and pain of Mr Pickwick's sojourn in the Fleet prison to the joy of reconciliation which takes place in its final chapters. Beneath the tissue of episodes which forms the surface structure of the novel lies a deeper structure which is concerned with the comic unmasking of villainy and the triumphant demonstration of the nature of goodness, of which the foremost characteristic is love. These deeper themes are obvious to the careful reader but the surface of the novel contains irresistible delights. Here is how Dickens presents Mr Pickwick on the trail of Alfred Jingle whom he believes to be ensnaring yet another young girl. Caught in a thunderstorm, Mr Pickwick knocks on the door of a house where he expects to be admitted by Mr Jingle's man-servant:

> He walked on tip-toe across the moist gravel, and tapped at the door. He held his breath, and listened at the key-hole. No reply: very odd. Another knock. He listened again. There was a low whispering inside, and then a voice cried –
>
> 'Who's there?'
>
> 'That's not Job,' thought Mr Pickwick, hastily drawing himself straight up against the wall again. 'It's a woman.'
>
> He had scarcely had time to form this conclusion, when a window above stairs was thrown up, and three or four female voices repeated the query – 'Who's there?'
>
> Mr Pickwick dared not move hand or foot. It was clear that the whole establishment was roused. He made up his mind to remain where he was, until the alarm had subsided: and then by a supernatural effort, to get over the wall, or perish in the attempt.
>
> Like all Mr Pickwick's determinations, this was the best that could be made under the circumstances; but, unfortunately, it was founded upon the assumption that they would not venture to open the door again. What was his discomfiture, when he heard the chain and bolts withdrawn, and saw the door slowly opening, wider and wider! He retreated into the corner, step by step; but do what he would, the interposition of his own person prevented its being opened to its utmost width.

'Who's there?' screamed a numerous chorus of treble voices from the staircase inside, consisting of the spinster lady of the establishment, three teachers, five female servants, and thirty boarders, all half-dressed, and in a forest of curl-papers.

Of course Mr Pickwick didn't say who *was* there: and then the burden of the chorus changed into – 'Lor'! I am so frightened.'

'Cook,' said the lady abbess, who took care to be on the top stair, the very last of the group – 'Cook, why don't you go a little way into the garden?'

'Please, ma'am, I don't like,' responded the cook.

'Lor', what a stupid thing that cook is!' said the thirty boarders.

'Cook,' said the lady abbess, with great dignity; 'don't answer me, if you please. I insist upon your looking into the garden immediately.'

Here the cook began to cry, and the housemaid said it was 'a shame!', for which partisanship she received a month's warning on the spot.

'Do you hear, cook?' said the lady abbess, stamping her foot impatiently.

'Don't you hear your missis, cook?' said the three teachers.

'What an impudent thing, that cook is!' said the thirty boarders.

The unfortunate cook, thus strongly urged, advanced a step or two, and holding her candle just where it prevented her from seeing anything at all, declared there was nothing there, and it must have been the wind. The door was just going to be closed in consequence, when an inquisitive boarder, who had been peeping between the hinges, set up a fearful screaming, which called back the cook and the housemaid and all the more adventurous, in no time.

'What is the matter with Miss Smithers?' said the lady abbess, as the aforesaid Miss Smithers proceeded to go into hysterics of four young lady power.

'Lor', Miss Smithers dear,' said the other nine-and-twenty boarders.

'Oh, the man – the man – behind the door!' screamed Miss Smithers.

The lady abbess no sooner heard this appalling cry, than she retreated to her own bedroom, double-locked the door, and fainted away comfortably. The boarders, and the teachers, and the servants, fell back upon the stairs, and upon each other; and never was such a screaming, and fainting, and struggling, beheld. In the midst of the tumult, Mr Pickwick emerged from his concealment, and presented himself amongst them.

'Ladies – dear ladies', said Mr Pickwick.

This episode shows how far the novel has come since the bald and rapid recital of events which we found in *Gil Blas* and *Roderick Random*.

Critics have become accustomed to speak of the theatricality of Dickens's presentation of his material. Here the organisation of the scene is almost operatic. Committed feminists may deplore Dickens's portrayal of the 'ladies' here: they are ranged on the stairs like a chorus (Dickens surely uses the word advisedly) out of the operas of Gilbert and Sullivan,* in which a similarly ambiguous attitude to women combines conventional masculine worship with a scarcely disguised disdain. As is frequently the case when Dickens means to be funny, individual existence is deliberately denied to the people involved: the headmistress becomes 'the lady abbess' – a theatrical figure at the head of her defenceless band. The cries of the residents are transformed into an operatic set piece for chorus and soloist with interpolated passages for a comic trio of teachers, and dramatic duets between headmistress and servants. The words of the girls have the function of a muttered refrain ('Lor' I am so frightened/Lor', what a stupid thing that cook is/What an impudent thing, that cook is/Lor', Miss Smithers dear' – notice how similar the rhythm of each phrase is; notice, too, the verbal resemblances between them). Although Dickens is getting as much humour as he can out of the sexual impropriety in which Mr Pickwick is involved (his timid knock on the door is comically transformed into the sacrilegious invasion of a house of nuns), what gives life to the passage is Dickens's gift of language. He compels his readers to attend to his style, the rhythm and movement of which are skilfully controlled by the voice of the narrator.

In being transferred from Spain to France, from France to England the tradition of the picaresque novel lost its keen satirical edge. It no longer presented the view of the social outcast; it became episodic rather than picaresque. Dickens, who had begun his writing career under the influence of his own interpretation of the tradition, began to find that this free-wheeling method of composition no longer served his purpose. It was no longer enough to say, as he had allowed Mr Pickwick to say, 'And now . . . the only question is, Where shall we go next?' In recent times novels have been written which bear more resemblance to the original conception of the picaresque novel: the conception of the hero as outsider has led to a revival of the *picaro* figure who lives on the margins of society, views it cynically or critically, and moves around it scrutinising its institutions and influential figures. Among them may be mentioned *The Invisible Man* (1952) by Ralph Ellison (*b*.1914), *The Adventures of Augie March* (1953) by Saul Bellow (*b*.1915), *The Confessions of Felix Krull* (1954) by Thomas Mann (1875–1955) and *The Ginger Man* (1955) by J. P. Donleavy (*b*.1926).

*Sir William Schwenk Gilbert (1836–1911) and Sir Arthur Sullivan (1842–1900) wrote and composed the music for a series of comic operettas satirising English society which have been popular from their first performance to the present day.

The novel in letters (the epistolary novel)

Mention has already been made of the fashion which arose briefly in the eighteenth century for presenting the novel in the form of a series of letters. One of the problems of this new form of writing was that, although it was fiction, it appeared to insist upon its truth. Readers required considerably more sophistication than could be relied upon at that time to perform the imaginative act of accepting that fiction could be a kind of truth. Perhaps any new form of communication requires a new kind of sophistication from its audiences: the fictitious 'news-broadcast' in the thirties by the film-maker, Orson Welles ((b.1915), about the invasion of New York by Martians is a modern instance of the failure to distinguish between truth and fiction. In the eighteenth century some authors claimed merely to be secretaries, or editors ('ghost writers', we might now say) who had put the verbal narratives of the principal character into written form. As Daniel Defoe wrote in the preface to *Robinson Crusoe* (1719), 'The editor believes the thing [his novel] to be a just history of fact; neither is there any appearance of fiction in it'. The equivocation in the final clause was perhaps enough to save Defoe's conscience; it is not clear how much it deceived the reader.

A different method of achieving authenticity was to allow it to be understood that the author was simply the editor of a bundle of letters from various hands which threw light on an interesting 'human' situation. Letter-writing was a significant part of eighteenth-century life, as it had been of the classical world of Rome and the Roman Empire from which the letters of Cicero and Pliny had been preserved. The observant letters of Madame de Sévigné (1626–96) to her daughter, full of personal, literary and social news, had been published in 1725. The English poet, Alexander Pope (1688–1744), had gone to considerable trouble to publish his own letters in 1737. He was inspired by the poignant letters of Héloïse and Abélard, unfortunate lovers of the twelfth century, to write his poem, 'Eloisa to Abelard' (1717) in which occur the following lines:

> Heav'n first taught letters for some wretch's aid,
> Some banish'd lover, or some captive maid;
> They live, they speak, they breathe what love inspires
> Warm from the soul, and faithful to its fires,
> The virgin's wish without her fears impart,
> Excuse the blush, and pour out all the heart.

Whether or not Samuel Richardson, whose *Pamela* (1740) and *Clarissa* (1748) had a profound effect upon his English and European readers, was influenced by these lines, they suggest the value of the letter to the novelist. The letter form allows him an opportunity for immediate expression of the personal feelings of his characters, in which earlier novelists seemed not to be interested. As one of Richardson's contemporaries put it in a comment upon *Clarissa*,

> The writers of Novels and Romances have generally endeavoured to pick out the most pleasing stories; to pass over the dry parts in them; and to hurry the reader on from one striking event to another. Their only aim seems to be that of making a tissue of adventures, which by their strangeness and variety are meant only to surprise and please. Nature they have not much in view; and morality is often quite out of the question with them.
>
> Instead of following this way of writing, the author of *Clarissa* has attempted to give a plain and natural account of an affair that happened in a private family, just in the manner that it did happen. He has aimed solely at following Nature: and giving the sentiments of the persons concerned, just as they flowed warm from their hearts.

Clarissa is a long and elaborate novel in which the heroine, daughter of a wealthy family, is wooed by a profligate aristocrat, Robert Lovelace. Clarissa's family want her to marry a wealthy but disagreeable older man called Mr Solmes. She is abducted by Lovelace who attempts to seduce her and finally rapes her, while she is under the influence of drugs that he has given her. The relationship between Clarissa and Lovelace is complex: she is attracted to him; he loves her, though some quirk of his nature makes him wish to hurt her. Having degraded her, he wishes to be forgiven and wants to marry her. She refuses and, very slowly, dies a martyr to the combined cruelty of her lover and her family. There are two main sets of correspondents in the novel – Clarissa and her friend, Anna Howe, and Lovelace and his friend, Belford. This arrangement allows Richardson to take his readers into the inner thoughts of the main characters. It allows him to present the action of the novel through the eyes of each of them, and while one of them is explaining what is happening, to keep the reader in suspense about what the other is thinking and feeling. The letters in *Clarissa* are organised in very large groups: almost all the letters in the first of the four volumes of the novel (in the Everyman edition) are from the correspondence between Clarissa and her friend. At the end of the volume, when Lovelace has succeeded in enticing Clarissa to go away with him, we are given the correspondence between Lovelace and Belford instead.

From such a very lengthy novel, combining as it does prolixity and suspense, it is difficult to select a passage which will do justice to Richardson's imaginative power. A novel as long as *Clarissa* is likely to remain unread, but students of the novel ought to have some first-hand acquaintance with Richardson's work. Contact with it, however slight, will convince the reader that here is not merely a figure of historical importance. Richardson is a vivid and engrossing writer, whose novels would be difficult to put down if we had the leisure and the patience to take them up. Here is a description from one of Clarissa's letters of how her sister Bella broke the news that a family conference had decided that Clarissa must marry Mr Solmes:

Obedience without reserve is required of you, Clary. My papa is justly incensed that you should *presume* to dispute his will, and to make conditions with him. He knows what is best for you; and as you own matters are gone a great way between this hated Lovelace and you, they will believe nothing you say; except you will give the one *only* instance, that will put them out of doubt of the sincerity of your promises.

What, child, are you surprised? Cannot you speak? Then, it seems, you had expected a different issue, had you? Strange that you could! With all your acknowledgements and confessions, so creditable to your *noted prudence*!

I was indeed speechless for some time: my eyes were even fixed, and ceased to flow. But, upon the hard-hearted Bella's proceeding with her airs of insult, indeed I *was* mistaken, said I; indeed I was! For in you, Bella, I expected, I hoped for, a sister –

What! interrupted she, with all your mannerly flings, and your despising airs, did you expect that I was capable of telling stories for you? Did you think that when I was asked my own opinion of the sincerity of your declarations, I could not tell them *how far matters had gone between you and your fellow* [Lovelace]? When the intention is to bend that stubborn will of yours to your duty, do you think I would deceive them? Do you think I would encourage them to call you down, to contradict all that I should have *invented* in your favour?

Well, well, Bella; I am the less obliged to you; that's all. I was willing to think that I had still a brother and sister. But I find I am mistaken. *Pretty Mopsa-eyed soul*, was her expression! And was it willing to think it had still a *brother* and *sister*? And why don't you go on, Clary? (mocking my half-weeping accent) I thought too I had a *father* and *mother*, two uncles and an *aunt*: but *I am mis-taken that's all* – come, Clary, say this, and it will in part be true, because you have thrown off their authority, and because you respect one vile wretch more than them all.

How have I deserved this at your hands, sister? But I will only say, I pity you.

And with that disdainful air too, Clary! None of that bridled neck! None of your scornful pity, girl! I beseech you!

This sort of behaviour is natural to you, surely, Bella! What *new* talents does it discover in you! But proceed – if it be a pleasure to you, proceed, Bella. And since I must not pity *you*, I will pity *myself*: for nobody else will.

Because you don't, said she –

Hush, Bella, interrupting her, *because I don't deserve it* – I know you were going to say so. I will say as you say in everything; and that's the way to please you.

Then say, Lovelace is a villain.

So I will, when I think him so.

Then you don't think him so?

Indeed I don't. *You* did not always, Bella.

And what, Clary, mean you by that? (bristling up to me) Tell me what you mean by that reflection?

Tell me why you call it a reflection? What did I say?

Thou art a provoking creature – but what say you to two or three duels of that wretch's?

I can't tell what to say, unless I knew the occasions.

Do you justify duelling at all?

I do not: neither can I help his duelling.

Will you go down and humble that stubborn spirit of yours to your mamma?

I said nothing.

Shall I conduct your ladyship down? (offering to take my declined hand)

What! not vouchsafe to answer me?

I turned from her in silence.

What! turn your back upon me too! Shall I bring up your mamma to you, love (following me, and taking my struggling hand) What! not speak yet! Come, my sullen, silent dear, speak one word to me – you must say *two* very soon to Mr Solmes, I can tell you that.

Perhaps this passage gives some of the flavour of Richardson's novel; it may remind us that some of the pleasure of the novel form was supposed to lie in its sheer length. The novelist, like the gossip, was expected to revel in detail. As we saw in considering the passage from *The Pickwick Papers*, the novel is essentially dramatic in form. But here the novelist is much less obviously in control of the presentation of the scene; there is no narrator to stage-manage the development of this angry little scene. The dialogue between Bella and Clarissa has a form that imitates the flow of dialogue in real life. A formal exchange of views grows sharper and more abrupt. As the discussion between the two sisters grows warmer, now one, now the other, asserts herself. Their mocking mimicry of one another is a perfectly recognisable feature of sisterly quarrels today. 'Whatever you say, I'll say too,' says Clarissa in effect. And the quarrel breaks into a verbal slanging-match in which the sisters exchange sentences as their less civilised counterparts might exchange blows. Richardson's control of the rhythm of the scene is masterly. Bella is first of all triumphant over Clarissa because she has on her lips the pronouncements of the family council which she comes to tell her sister about. The formal sentences she utters have the authority and gravity of her father's style. As proof of Clarissa's severance from Lovelace, they demand that she marries Mr Solmes. It is only when Bella begins to speak in her own tones that the coarse malice of her character comes through. Notice her insistent use of the first personal pronoun; notice the arrogant self-assertion of her rhetorical questions to Clarissa. When Clarissa tries to remonstrate, she breaks out into a heartless mockery of Clarissa's tearful attempts to touch her sister's feelings. Bella's sarcasm strikes some answering fire from Clarissa. The speech rhythms tighten to a repartee which displays the sinews of the English language. Phrases fly between the two girls like hard-driven tennis balls. ('Then say, Lovelace is a villain/So I will when I think him so.') Richardson is so sure that his readers will follow the patterns of his language that he reduces to a minimum his guidance as to who is speaking. The tones of voice of the two girls draw closer together until Clarissa is as disdainful and disobliging as Bella, and 'Clary' and 'Bella' are all that is needed to tell them apart. Bella, the reader might think, wins in the end, reducing Clarissa to silence, threatening her with the two words of the marriage service which will make her Mr Solmes's wife. But has she defeated Clarissa's 'stubborn spirit', or is Clarissa's silence simply the clearest sign of her resolve?

The epistolary novel had a brief but intense European vogue at the end of the eighteenth century. Jean-Jacques Rousseau (1712–78) employed it in his *Julie ou la nouvelle Héloise* (1761), Smollett used it cleverly in his last novel, *Humphry Clinker* (1771), J. W. von Goethe (1749–1832) in *The Sorrows of Young Werther* (1774), Fanny Burney (1752–1840) in her first brilliantly successful novel *Evelina* (1778) which described the excitements high society held for a young girl entering the world at eighteen. Looking back on the form from the vantage point of 1824, Sir Walter Scott (1771–1832) said of it in his novel *Redgauntlet* (which opens with an exchange of letters between two sharply contrasted young men):

> The advantage of laying before the reader, in the words of the actors themselves, the adventures which we must otherwise have narrated in our own has given great popularity to the publication of epistolary correspondence, as practised by various great authors, and by ourselves in the preceding chapters. Nevertheless a genuine correspondence of this kind (and Heaven forfend it should be in any respect sophisticated by interpolations of our own!) can seldom be found to contain all in which it is necessary to instruct the reader for his full comprehension of the story. Also it must often happen that

various prolixities and redundancies occur in the course of an interchange of letters which must hang as a dead weight on the progress of the narrative.

(It is interesting that as late as 1824 Sir Walter Scott still believed that he must still maintain the pretence, even if ironically, that the letters upon which his novel were based were genuine!)

The clumsiness of the novel-in-letters, as Scott suggests, brought about its disappearance. The artificiality it imposed on the writer was no compensation for the immediate entry it offered into the hearts and minds of the characters. In France an infantry officer, Choderlos de Laclos (1741–1803) used it to great effect in his only novel, *Les Liaisons Dangereuses* (1782), which describes in a series of letters between two separated cynical lovers the progress of their seduction of an innocent pair of young people. Laclos brilliantly exploits the dramatic possibilities of the form and the sense it conveys of the narrowly concentrated personal point of view of the letter-writers, isolated, self-occupied, ignorant of, and indifferent to, the demands of society and the interests of those whom they have selected as their victims. Laclos' novel was long thought to be scandalous; it still has power to suggest the force of calculated human evil. Thereafter, this form of fiction fell out of fashion. In 1793–4, Jane Austen (1775–1817) wrote her first attempt at fiction, *Lady Susan*, in this style, but the book was not published in her life-time and she did not repeat the experiment, although she frequently uses letters in her novels, especially to reveal secrets which are essential to her plot. To Richardson, however, she owed much of her understanding of human nature and something of her fictional presentation of it. It is perhaps instructive to compare the passage which has been quoted from *Clarissa* with the following passage from *Emma* (1816) where Jane Austen uses just the kind of dramatic technique which Richardson pioneered. At this point, Harriet Smith, Emma's young friend and protégée has just come to give Emma the news (which she already knows) that their friend, Jane Fairfax, has become engaged to Frank Churchill, with whom Emma mistakenly believes Harriet to be in love:

> 'Well, Miss Woodhouse!' cried Harriet, coming eagerly into the room – 'is not this the oddest news that ever was?'
>
> 'What news do you mean?' replied Emma, unable to guess, by look or voice, whether Harriet could indeed have received any hint.
>
> 'About Jane Fairfax .... that Jane Fairfax and Mr Frank Churchill are to be married, and that they have been privately engaged to one another this long while. How very odd!'
>
> It was indeed, so odd; Harriet's behaviour was so extremely odd, that Emma did not know how to understand it. Her character

appeared absolutely changed. She seemed to propose showing no agitation, or disappointment, or peculiar concern in the discovery. Emma looked at her, quite unable to speak.

'Had you any idea,' cried Harriet, 'of his being in love with her? – You, perhaps, might. – You (blushing as she spoke) who can see into everybody's heart; but nobody else –'

'Upon my word,' said Emma, 'I begin to doubt my having any such talent. Can you seriously ask me, Harriet, whether I imagined him attached to another woman at the very time that I was – tacitly, if not openly – encouraging you to give way to your own feelings? – I never had the slightest suspicion, till within the last hour, of Mr Frank Churchill's having the least regard for Jane Fairfax. You may be very sure that if I had, I should have cautioned you accordingly.'

'Me!' cried Harriet, colouring and astonished. 'Why should you caution me? – You do not think I care about Mr Frank Churchill.'

'I am delighted to hear you speak so stoutly on the subject,' replied Emma, smiling; 'but you do not mean to deny there was a time – and not very distant either – when you gave me to understand that you did care about him?'

'Him! – never, never. Dear Miss Woodhouse, how could you so mistake me?' turning away distressed.

'Harriet!' cried Emma, after a moment's pause – 'What do you mean? Good Heaven! What do you mean? Mistake you! – Am I to suppose then? –'

She could not speak another word. – Her voice was lost; and she sat down, waiting in great terror till Harriet should answer.

Harriet, who was standing at some distance, and with face turned from her, did not immediately say anything; and when she did speak, it was in a voice nearly as agitated as Emma's.

Here Jane Austen also uses the rapid asides – almost like stage-directions – which Richardson used to indicate emotion and attitude. However, the dialogue here is much faster, the drama much more condensed, than in our example from *Clarissa*. Jane Austen clearly differentiates her two characters by their mode of speech. Emma's sentences are much more carefully controlled than Harriet's, which are jerky, repetitive, hesitant, unfinished. In Emma's last speech, however, her fear that Harriet is about to confess to being in love with Mr Knightley releases a degree of emotion that shakes Emma's self-control. Jane Austen uses a number of devices here which remind us more of stage-craft than of narrative. She concentrates on the dialogue, stripping away narrative to the conventional speech verbs ('cried', 'replied') accompanied only by an indication of tone or mood. She also clearly indicates the relative postures of the speakers: Harriet, standing some distance from Emma with averted eyes, is confused, guilty perhaps, unable to remain in full communication with her. Every verbal and non-verbal sign indicates mutual misunderstanding.

By 1816 novelists have managed to combine the controlled flow of narrative with vividly dramatised scenes. In *Emma* the narrator is so close to Emma that to pass from the dramatised dialogue to the narrative commentary is rather like moving from the external space of action and event to the internal space of thought, motivation and decision. Jane Austen has retained the vivacity of feeling which Clarissa gave to her own account of her predicament, and has gained a freedom of action to tell the story in her own way, unconstrained by the point of view of the letter-writer. The novel-in-letters leads directly to the dramatic novel.

Readers who would like to see how modern forms of communication such as letters, telegrams and telephone calls can be pressed into the service of the novelist, should look at *An Accidental Man* (1971) by Iris Murdoch (*b.*1919). Saul Bellow (*b.*1915) has made his hero a compulsive letter-writer in *Herzog* (1964) and John Barth (*b.*1931) has written a pastiche of the eighteenth-century form in his huge novel *Letters* (1979).

The novel as history

At the end of the eighth chapter of the First Part of *Don Quixote* (1605), Don Quixote is fighting the servant of a lady travelling by coach to Seville, whom the knight has taken to be a princess kidnapped by sorcerers. The chapter ends at an interesting point: Don Quixote stands with sword raised, firmly resolved to split the servant in half; the servant waits to meet the blow. And Cervantes says:

> But at this point of crisis, the author of the history leaves the battle in suspense, spoiling the whole episode. The excuse he offers is that he could find nothing more written about these achievements of Don Quixote than what has been already told. It is true the second author of this work [Cervantes himself] was unwilling to believe that so interesting a history could have been allowed to lapse into oblivion, or that learned persons in La Mancha could have been so undiscerning as not to preserve in their archives or registries some documents referring to this famous knight. Since such was his conviction, he did not despair of discovering the conclusion of this pleasant history.

Don Quixote is one of those great books which are more referred to than read. It has suffered the fate of *Robinson Crusoe* (1719) and *Gulliver's Travels* (1726) in that most readers first come across them in their youth in abridged versions which do little justice to the works themselves, but which leave them with the belief that they know what the books are about. *Don Quixote* is one of the greatest works of European literature; it stands on a boundary between the medieval and the modern world; it acts as mediator between incompatible visions of the world, between a willingness to believe in the extraordinary and the marvellous and a more down-to-earth determination not to be duped. Cervantes explores with insight and sympathy the relationship between the power which human beings possess (and which other members of the animal kingdom have to a much smaller extent) to see things as they are not, or as they might be, and the constraints of the world of things and circumstances in which everything is what it is, and nothing else. The characters of Don Quixote and Sancho Panza, his squire, may be seen as representing two permanent aspects of the human mind – its capacity for conjecture and supposition and its ability to test the leaps of imagination against some standard of reality and truth.

Cervantes presents himself as 'the second author' of *Don Quixote*; he wants his reader to believe that he has *discovered* the story of a man whose brains were turned by reading too many romances about the knights of chivalry so that he came to believe he was a knight himself. But the sources were defective: Cervantes has been relying (so he tells us) on a fragment of Don Quixote's story which has come to an end. What is he to do? He has no doubt that Don Quixote was a real person (although the first words of the novel, 'In a village of La Mancha', are a quotation from an old ballad), so it may be that people of his village still remember him. From the beginning of the novel, then, the 'real' Don Quixote is enclosed in the fictionalised village of La Mancha and Cervantes has begun the teasing game of mixing fact and fiction which novelists have practised ever since.

Even at the outset of his journey, Don Quixote looks forward to the fortunate author who will relate his story to the world:

> As our new-fledged adventurer paced along, he kept talking to himself. 'Who knows', he said, 'whether in time to come, when the veracious history of my famous deeds is made known, the sage who writes it, when he has to set forth my first sally in the early morning, may not do it after this fashion?
>
> 'Scarce had the rubicund Apollo spread o'er the face of the broad spacious earth the golden threads of his bright hair, scarce had the little birds of painted plumage attuned their notes to hail . . . the coming of the rosy Dawn . . . when the renowned Don Quixote of La Mancha . . . mounted his celebrated steed Rocinante and began to traverse the ancient and famous Fields of Montiel', which in fact he actually was traversing.

By setting Don Quixote's idea of how his journey might be described within the very different words which he has used to describe it, Cervantes achieves an effect of depth which increases our sense of the character's reality. Don Quixote's prophecy that his exploits will be recorded has, after all, been realised. He expects to be memorialised in the poetic language appropriate to chivalric romances, a style which decreases the reader's sense that what is reported actually happened. In fact, Cervantes reports his doings in plain prose, which tends to increase the credibility of what has been reported.

It is not, however, in local gossip or in the archives of La Mancha that Cervantes discovers Don Quixote's history and finds out what happened to the threatened servant of the supposedly kidnapped princess. One day in a market-place in Toledo, says Cervantes, he found some notebooks and odd papers written in Arabic which a passer-by, who knew the language, translated for him. This is what he says:

> When I . . . put the book into his hand, he opened it in the middle and read a little. Then he began to laugh. I asked him what he was laughing at, and he replied that it was at something in a note written in the margin of the book. I asked him to tell me what it was.
> 'In the margin, as I told you', he replied, still laughing, 'is written: "This Dulcinea del Toboso so often mentioned in this history, had, they say, the best hand of any woman in La Mancha for salting pigs."'
> When I heard Dulcinea del Toboso named, I was struck with surprise and amazement, for it occurred to me at once that these notebooks contained the history of Don Quixote. With this idea I urged him to read the beginning, and he did so, turning the Arabic into Castilian at sight. He told me it meant, "History of Don Quixote of La Mancha, written by Cide Hamete Benengeli," an Arab historian.

And so a third author appears in the scene! The notebook, Cervantes tells us, even contained a picture of Don Quixote's battle with the servant, and so, finally, we hear how the fight between them ended.

Some readers may have found Cervantes's way of telling his story merely tiresome; others may have been as fascinated by it as perhaps they were by that famous advertisement which shows a picture of a boy eating one of his favourite brands of biscuits from a box on which . . . . Most of us have at some time been intrigued by the reduplication of images which takes place when we look in a mirror and see the reflection of another mirror in which we are reflected looking in a mirror. Some such unsettling effect is conveyed by the references that *Don Quixote* makes to itself: it achieves perhaps a double effect. From one point of view it increases the reader's sense of respect for the sophistication of the author. He has the sleight-of-hand of a conjuror who can create illusions which have a convincing air of truth. Yet he can play tricks with his audience, assuring them that he is offering them fiction, while making them believe that what he is telling is fact. On the other hand, the effect which he produces is strangely three-dimensional. In placing himself between the reader and the first and third authors of the story of Don Quixote, Cervantes increases his own reliability as a narrator. He is no longer a simple story-teller: in presenting a translation of Cide Hamete Benengeli's history, he offers himself as a critical historian, skilfully separating with resourcefulness and integrity fact from fiction, falsehood from truth.

The fiction which claims to be treated seriously as history is one of the most persistent and most influential types of the novel. As has been explained earlier, Daniel Defoe wrote fictions of this kind, usually narrated in the first person, the style of which carried some suggestion that behind the narrative was hidden an authentic human being. Here, for example, is Defoe's Colonel Jack, recollecting his feelings of guilt after his first major exploit as a juvenile thief:

> As soon as it was day, I got out of the hole we lay in, and rambled abroad into the fields, towards Stepney, and there I mused and considered what I should do with this money, and many a time I wished that I had not had it, for after all my ruminating upon it, and what course I should take with it, or where I should put it, I could not hit upon any one thing, or any possible method to secure it, and it perplexed me so, that at last, as I said just now, I sat down and cried heartily.
>
> When my crying was over, the case was the same; I had the money still, and what to do with it I could not tell, at last it came into my head, that I would look out for some hole in a tree, and see to hide it there, till I should have occasion for it: big with this discovery, as I then thought it, I began to look about me for a tree; but there were no trees in the fields about Stepney . . . and if there were any that I began to look narrowly at, the fields were so full of people, that they would see if I went to hide anything there, and I thought the people eyed me as it was, and that two men in particular followed me, to see what I intended to do.
>
> This drove me further off, and I crossed the road at Mile-End, and in the middle of the town I went down a lane that goes away to the Blind Beggar's at Bethnal-Green; when I came a little way in the lane, I found a foot-path over the fields, and in those fields several trees for my turn, as I thought; at last one tree had a little hole in it, pretty high out of my reach, and I climbed up to the tree to get to it, and when I came there, I put my hand in, and found (as I thought) a place very fit, so I placed my treasure there, and was mighty well satisfied with it; but behold, putting my hand in again to lay it more commodiously, as I thought, of a sudden it slipped away from me, and I found the tree was hollow, and my little parcel was fallen in quite out of my reach, and how far it might go in, I knew not; so that, in a word, my money was

quite gone, irrecoverably lost, there could be no room, so much as to hope ever to see it again for it was a vast great tree.

As young as I was, I was now sensible what a fool I was before, that I could not think of ways to keep my money, but I must come thus far to throw it into a hole where I could not reach it; well, I thrust my hand quite up to my elbow, but no bottom was to be found, or any end of the hole or cavity; I got a stick off of the tree and thrust it in a great way, but all was one; then I cried, nay, I roared out, I was in such a passion, then I got down the tree again, then up again, and thrust my hand again till I scratched my arm and made it bleed, and cried all the while most violently: then I began to think I had not so much as a half-penny of it left for a half-penny roll, and I was a hungry, and then I cried again: then I came away in despair, crying, and roaring like a little boy that had been whipped, then I went back again to the tree, and up the tree again, and thus I did several times.

The last time I had gotten up the tree, I happened to come down not on the same side that I went up and came down before, but on the other side of the tree, and on the other side of the bank also; and behold the tree had a great open place in the side of it close to the ground, as old hollow trees often have; and looking into the open place, to my inexpressible joy, there lay my money, and my linen rag, all wrapped up just as I had put it into the hole.

This complete episode from Defoe's *Colonel Jack* (1722) is worth considering in several ways. Suppose, first of all, that it is an authentic narrative, what would convince us of its authenticity? First, the episode is a typical example of human experience; it is built up out of regrets and plans and expectations and disappointments. It must be granted that the narrator, if authentic, has a high degree of skill as a story-teller. The smooth flow of the narrative, never resting for a moment and having all the appearance of unstudied spontaneity, arranges itself beautifully into four clearly marked sequences: a moment of despondency followed by fear; a moment of successfully accomplished action; the reversal and frustration of that action which leads to frantic unsuccessful activity; and the chance solution of the difficulty which has arisen. The skill of the telling of the story is masked by the simplicity of the language. The repetitions of the phrase 'as I thought' have that convincing air of truthfulness which we associate with the careful re-telling of a story just as it happened. The repetition of the word 'again' has the careless conversational quality of speech that is more intent on being exact than being elegant. The story is coherent; it is detailed; it refers in a convincing way to places which can still be identified; it is told in sentences which carry the rhythms and vocabulary of everyday English.

If we remember, however, that it is not an authentic story but a piece of fiction contrived by Defoe, we can at once see the artistry of the narrative. This experience is so typical of human experience that it is exemplary; its typicality carries a message. It reminds us of the fluctuating, transient quality of human emotion; it analyses the morality and the psychology of theft with a sharpness which we would scarcely expect of the narrator himself. Although the story has the appearance of naturalness, once we are aware of its status as fiction, we can see more clearly how skilfully it has been designed to present a carefully structured action in miniature.

Defoe offers us an example of a learning experience: the little boy's feelings are concentrated entirely upon the pleasure and pain which govern his appetites and desires. The money has brought unpleasant feelings of guilt, but the need for money (and, in his case, the necessity of theft) is a natural consequence of the need for food. Although Colonel Jack has been a thief from necessity, when he tells his story he is the colonel of his regiment. In looking back on his earlier self, he is clarifying his ideas about whether stealing is always wrong. The older man is able to measure the distance between his present self and the urchin he remembers. Out of his youthful guilt and hunger and puzzlement at the unpredictability of the natural world he has created a life which is ordered, purposeful and mature. Under the rags of the street urchin there lay a rescuable human soul. The point of Defoe's narrative is to trace how the rescue was effected.

Or, at least, it ought to be. Part of the dissatisfaction readers have felt about Defoe's novels is that they are too diffuse. The clarity which we have seen in this detail of *Colonel Jack* is perhaps less obvious in the novel as a whole. History and moral example may easily appear as two sides of the same coin of narrative, but if the novel is to be convincing as an exemplary tale it must be more consistent than Defoe's novels usually are. Despite their authenticity, they remain episodic, unco-ordinated; they are chronicles, rather than history. If the novel is to be seen as history, it must be more than a series of events. Indeed, the first critical student of literature, the Greek philosopher Aristotle (384–322BC) thought that literature might go further than history in treating human affairs in a serious way. He believed it to be 'more philosophical' than history. As the American scholar John Gassner puts it in his introduction to S. H. Butcher's translation of *The Poetics*:

> Art creates an idea of order where, to the inartistic or unphilosophical observer, life is only a whirl of action and chaos of emotion. In literature ... the writer creates a logical sequence and causal connection of events. The crude matter of life assumes significance from the shaping hand of the artist.*

Aristotle's Theory of Poetry and Fine Art, ed. by S. H. Butcher, with a prefatory essay by John Gassner, 4th edn., Dover Publications Inc., New York, 1951, p. xli.

Of course, serious history itself could be written in this larger, more philosophical way. Historians could see themselves not just as purveyors of fact but as analysts of trends or tendencies in human affairs. Within the random flux of circumstance they might discern a pattern. Aristotle was writing before the novel had made any claim to be treated as a serious literary form. When Henry Fielding (1707–54) began to write novels, having received a classical education himself, he turned naturally to the theory and practice of those writers who were believed in the eighteenth century to have contributed most to European literature. It was against the models of classical literature – in particular, the epics of Greece and Rome – that he believed his new kind of writing should be judged. If he was writing history, it should be history in the larger sense: his novels would present human beings in situations which illustrated permanent truths about the nature of man.

Fielding's first novel *Joseph Andrews* (1742) had been prompted by Richardson's *Pamela*. *Pamela* had told in an exchange of letters the story of a simple but honest servant girl who, on the death of her mistress, was subjected to what would now be called sexual harassment by her late mistress's son, Mr B—. Kept a prisoner in one of his houses under the supervision of a very disagreeable housekeeper, Pamela manages to elude her master's attentions and to convert his lust into love and an offer of marriage. Richardson's novel was a popular success but its blend of priggishness and pruriency caused some readers to despise it. To some, Pamela was a schemer who was quite prepared to trade her sexual favours in return for marriage and a secure life: her talk of virtue was hypocrisy. *Joseph Andrews* – supposedly the story of Pamela's brother – began as a parody of Richardson's novel: Joseph was to be a male prude. But under Fielding's hand it developed rather differently and it is now interesting as much for what Fielding says about the form of the novel as for the story which he tells.

The full title of the novel is *The History/of the/Adventures/of/Joseph Andrews/and of his Friend/Mr Abraham Adams./ Written in Imitation of/the Manner of Cervantes/Author of Don Quixote.* Fielding finds the ancestry for his novel – 'this kind of writing, which I do not remember to have seen hitherto attempted in our language', as he puts it in the Preface – in *Don Quixote* and the classical epic. His novel is a 'comic epic in prose'. Unfortunately, the comic epic which Homer was believed to have written had been lost, so that there was no model for the kind of writing Fielding had in mind. *His* epic would be comic, his characters of inferior rank to the kings and heroes of epic poetry, and his language humorous. Comic epic was not to be merely a burlesque or caricature of serious epic (as the mock-heroic *Rape of the Lock*, 1714, by Alexander Pope had been). It was to have its own point and purpose, namely, the presentation and exposure of affected and ridiculous people, who were likely to be motivated by hypocrisy or vanity. The comic epic would take its subjects from life and would 'follow Nature': though the subjects would be treated in a comic way, they would not be distorted. Fielding had no wish to appear cruel or heartless. What was intrinsically evil in life (human degradation or deformity or misfortune) could never be a subject for laughter. As he put it, 'Great vices are the proper object of our detestation, smaller faults of our pity: but affectation appears to me the only true source of the ridiculous.' On these grounds, of course, Pamela's affectations of purity were a proper target of ridicule.

Fielding begins *Joseph Andrews* by blurring the distinction between fact and fiction, as Cervantes had done before him. He says that a principal function of the writer is to tell his readers about the lives of good men, so that they will serve as models of behaviour to a wider circle than those who know them personally. He cites the historians of Greece and Rome and 'in our language' 'the history of John the Great, who by his brave and heroic actions against men of large and athletic bodies, obtained the glorious appellation of "the Giant-Killer"'. So nursery tales about Jack the Giant-Killer are given the same dignity as Plutarch's *Lives*. Partly, of course, this is simply a joke, the bantering comparison of the solemn and the homely. Its serious point is that what links history and folk-tale is their common concern to offer their readers examples of good behaviour: the facts in each case are less significant than the ethical models which both kinds of story contain. In the same way, a genuine autobiography of the day is compared to Richardson's *Pamela*, which, says Fielding, has been 'communicated to us by an historian who borrows his lights [that is, 'gets his information'] from authentic papers and records'. So, *Joseph Andrews* is to be 'the authentic history' of Pamela's brother, who by keeping his sister's story in mind 'was chiefly enabled to preserve his purity in the midst of such great temptations'. What affectation can we then say was the object of Fielding's comic attention in this novel? The answer is curious: Fielding begins his novel by ridiculing the view that innocence is possible – would a young man-servant reject the advances of his mistress? – and ends by ridiculing the fashionably cynical view that innocent virtue is impossible. *Joseph Andrews* is an enquiry in the form of a novel into the character of the virtuous man.

Joseph Andrews is a simple enough tale: the chaste young hero, cast out of the service of Lady Booby (an aunt of Pamela's master, Mr B—, says Fielding), makes his way back to his village and his own true love, Fanny. On his way home, having been stripped and robbed by highway robbers, he meets Mr Abraham Adams, the curate of his village. Fanny, hearing of Joseph's misfortunes, sets out to find her sweetheart and, together, the clergyman and the young lovers make their way home. The substance of the narrative is what happens to them on the way. Their adventures are exemplary: Joseph and Fanny are handsome, innocent, and devoted to one another; Adams is a pattern of Christian saintliness in the eccentric form of an English clergyman, who not only knows what he believes but practises what he preaches. Fielding allows him to be subjected to the ludicrous humiliations which are likely to afflict the unworldly; but through his indignities his goodness shines steadily – and impressively. Fielding's narrative method is to contrast the unaffected goodness of his happy band with the greed, arrogance, aggression and deceit which surround them at every turn.

Fielding sees human beings as a great company of perennial types. He is a universal biographer who is not concerned with the petty detail of circumstance. Surface verisimilitude is of less consequence to him than the careful delineation of permanent features of the human character. As he says, 'I describe not men, but manners; not an individual, but a species!' To the objection that his characters are not drawn from real life, Fielding instances his picture of a craven, self-contained lawyer who makes malicious jokes out of the sufferings of others:

> The lawyer [he says] is not only alive, but hath been so these 4000 years; and I hope God will indulge his life as many yet to come. He hath not indeed confined himself to one profession, one religion, or one country; but when the first mean selfish creature appeared upon the human stage, who made self the centre of the whole creation, would give himself no pain, incur no danger, advance no money to assist or preserve his fellow-creatures; then was our lawyer born; and whilst such a person as I have described exists on earth, so long shall he remain upon it. It is therefore doing him [the novelist] little honour, to imagine he endeavours to mimick some obscure little fellow, because he happens to resemble him in one particular feature, or perhaps in his profession; whereas his [the novelist's] appearance in the world is calculated for much more general and noble purposes; not to expose one pitiful wretch to the small and contemptible circle of his acquaintance; but to hold the glass to thousands in their closets, that they may contemplate their deformity, and endeavour to reduce it, and thus by suffering private mortification may avoid public shame.

This warm and generous statement of his aims and duties as a writer throws light on the kind of historian Fielding thought the novelist should be. He is not simply a chronicler, still less an entertainer. He is a moralist who believes that through fiction – a fabricated tale which resembles the historian's narrative, but goes beyond it – he can trace permanent features of human nature. His story is experimental: it considers action and its likely consequence with a view to making recommendations about how people should behave. By his researches he can help his readers to distinguish the worthwhile from the trivial, the permanently satisfying from the superficially attractive.

Fielding's model for the novel has been profoundly influential. He saw its potentiality as a serious literary form. He recognised its flexibility: it could have the immediacy of drama and the leisurely detachment of the informal essay. The future task of the novelist might be to create a satisfactory form which would combine the virtues of these quite different literary techniques. Of greatest significance, perhaps, was the function he established for the novelist as active shaper and manipulator of the narrative. Fielding places his novel before the reader, as if inviting him to engage in a deeply serious game. The novel is 'only a novel', the characters simply puppets – but puppets which behave uncannily like 'real people'. When the puppet-master moves behind the curtain, his ability to focus our attention on what his creatures are doing is so great that we forget they are only marionettes. As narrator, Fielding can intervene, explain, move away from the detail of the story to the general truths which it was intended to illustrate. He can alter the distance between the three participants in the game – the narrator, the narrative and the reader. Now the actions of the characters completely occupy our attention; now narrator and reader confront one another talking about the game and its implications; now the narrator acts as unobtrusive commentator quietly describing what is going on. Fielding's kind of novel includes and goes beyond the picaresque novel; it includes the dramatic techniques which Richardson pioneered but differs from the Richardsonian novel by refusing to see the action and characters as a special case. Fielding's novels are didactic and moralistic, as well as witty and humorous. They are comprehensive and general; they are willing to take a broad panoramic view of how human beings behave; they aim to see life steadily and see it whole.

Although Fielding has much to say about the nature of the novel in *Joseph Andrews*, the action he invented does not quite measure up to the standards he set for this new form of literature. It is episodic, haphazard and lacking in the unity which Parson Adams believes is a necessary feature of the epic. The tone of *Joseph Andrews* changes when Fanny is brought on the scene. Joseph is no longer the naïve and inexperienced young man at risk amidst the temptations of city life; he is immediately transformed into a model of the honest affectionate attachment that a man can have for the girl he loves. The substance of the novel then becomes – how Joseph Andrews conveyed his treasure safely home. But Fielding finds it difficult to know what to do with them when they get there. He unashamedly produces an independent gentleman of modest means as Joseph's long-lost father. The reward of Joseph's goodness, the cynical may say, is his promotion to the middle class.

If Fielding is the historian of human types, Sir Walter Scott

(1771–1832) must be given credit for taking the novel as history a stage further. Fielding's view of history was limited. It left out of account the possibility of change or variation in the kinds of behaviour he regarded as admirable. Scott, on the other hand, inherited from the philosophers of eighteenth-century Scotland a view of history as a progressive movement which led to the establishment of new modes of behaviour and different concepts of what was admirable. In his greatest novels, *Waverley* (1814), *Old Mortality* (1816), *The Heart of Midlothian* (1818), *Rob Roy* (1818) and *Redgauntlet* (1824) Scott described and analysed transitional movements from one kind of society to another. In the course of such changes, Scott believed, virtues which were appropriate to one form of society were not necessarily appropriate to that which took its place. As society changed, the underlying inherited character traits of an individual might be modified by changes in the environment, by new standards of education or new social values. Joshua Geddes, the Quaker farmer in *Redgauntlet*, is the embodiment of peace and industry, though his ancestors have been independent soldiers of fortune. In a changed society Joshua shows how his heredity has been modified by circumstances, when he goes out unarmed to face an armed enemy. The valour of his ancestors walks in ways of peace. In other novels Scott tries to show how previously admirable qualities may now be out of place or even dangerous. So in *Waverley* the romantic devotion to the Jacobite cause and the loyalty to their chieftains shown by Highland clansmen threatens the stability of the commercial society which formed the basis of the union between England and Scotland. Clan loyalties belonged to a society in process of extinction: Scott loved and mourned these ancient virtues but saw their passing as a historical necessity.

Broad social and philosophical considerations of this kind can be seen in the novels of George Eliot (1819–80) and pre-eminently in *War and Peace* (1863–9) by Leo Tolstoy (1828–1910). The influence of Scott on the nineteenth-century European novel was extensive and can be seen in the novels of Honoré de Balzac (1799–1850) and Emile Zola (1840–1902). The modern Scottish novelist, Lewis Grassic Gibbon (pseud. of James Leslie Mitchell, 1901–35), in his trilogy collected in one volume as *A Scots Quair* (1946) studied the transition from an agrarian culture, steeped in the values of Victorian religion, to modern secular and commercial ways of life. Many modern African novelists, especially perhaps the Kenyan Ngugi wa Thiongo (*b*.1938) and the Ghanaian Ayi Kwei Armah (*b*.1939), have been drawn to the portrayal in fiction of the historical changes in their societies; the Nigerian Chinua Achebe (*b*.1930) offers in his *Things Fall Apart* a brief but very distinguished example of this type of novel. Also worth mentioning is the British novelist, Paul Scott (1920–78) whose *Raj Quartet* (1966–75) took as its subject the last years of British rule in India.

The anti-novel

A final section of this chapter must be devoted to the last significant novelist of the eighteenth century and to some of his descendants. Laurence Sterne was a rather eccentric clergyman who made no great mark on the world until he published in 1760 the first two books of *The Life and Opinions of Tristram Shandy*. Sterne's place in the history of the novel is now secure because of the literary quality of his novel, but he was long regarded as an oddity. In more recent times, however, novels of this type have almost become the norm rather than the exception.

If we consider the title of Sterne's novel alone, we may be led to expect something of the kind we have met before. It is modelled on the biography, so we might expect to be introduced to a man and his circle of acquaintances, to find out what kind of person he is and what his story has been. Nothing of this conventional kind happens in *Tristram Shandy*. The novel was originally published in two-volume instalments, except for the ninth and final volume, which was published on its own. Sterne meant to publish the book in yearly instalments, but as time went on the gaps between publication became longer. The creation of suspense and puzzled expectation is part of the design of the book. Indeed at one point in the novel, when he is describing 'the perplexities' of one of his characters, Uncle Toby, Sterne goes so far as to say:

> What these perplexities of my Uncle Toby were, – 'tis impossible for you to guess; – If you could, – I should blush; not as a relation, – not as a man, – not even as a woman, – but I should blush as an author; inasmuch as I set no small store by myself upon this very account, that my reader has never yet been able to guess at any-thing. And in this, Sir, I am of so nice and singular a humour, that if I thought you was able to form the least judgment or probable conjecture to yourself, of what was to come in the next page, – I would tear it out of my book.

The reader is left in no doubt about the narrator's independence of mind, though he may be astonished by the violence with which he expresses it. Sterne's method of telling his story is 'digressive': he is led from one topic to another in an apparently random way so that the story of Tristram Shandy never gets told.

The novel is narrated by Tristram himself. It is concerned with the events which take place in Tristram's family circle around the time of his birth. It is almost wholly devoted to two members of the Shandy family, Tristram's father, Walter Shandy, and his Uncle Toby, a retired military man who has fought in the Continental wars which preceded the Peace of Utrecht in 1713. Tristram's mother makes occasional brief, necessary appearances but she plays little part in what for want of a better word must be called the story. Four other characters are of some importance:

two, the widow Wadman and Corporal Trim, are connected with Uncle
Toby; the third, Dr Slop, is the doctor in attendance on the occasion of
Tristram's birth. The fourth, Yorick, the local clergyman, named after
the jester to the king in *Hamlet*, acts as an observer and chorus to much
of what goes on, though by the time the telling of the tale begins, he has
been dead for some years. He is, like Tristram, a version of Sterne
himself. Equally, four elements can be identified in the design of the
narrative: the first is the actual composition of the novel; the second is
the birth and early life of Tristram; the third is the story of Uncle Toby's
war experience, his war wound, the development of his hobby and the
courtship of the widow Wadman, the abrupt and unsuccessful
conclusion of which brings the novel to a close. The frequent
unpredictable digressions – a sermon of Yorick's, a solemn and
extensive oath of excommunication, a chapter on noses, an unfinished
tale of the king of Bohemia, and many others – make up the fourth.

Sterne uses some of the devices we are familiar with from the
epistolary novel. He writes some forty years after the events he is
describing, but the process of writing the book is represented as taking
place in a continuous present which means that the narrator cannot
quite be sure what is to happen from chapter to chapter. He makes it
clear that he has a general plan in mind but whether it will be realised is
not certain. Consider, for example, a passage from Volume III in which
he faces a moment of choice in the composition of his work. Corporal
Trim, Uncle Toby's servant, has arrived to announce that Dr Slop is
making a bridge in the kitchen: it is not, as Uncle Toby thinks, a bridge
for the model fortifications which he has laid out in his back garden,
being greatly interested in military strategy, it is an artificial bridge for
the newly-born Tristram's nose which Dr Slop has just flattened with his
forceps as he was delivering him in the bedroom upstairs. Here is how
Sterne puts the problem he confronts as an author:

> to understand how my Uncle Toby could mistake the bridge – I fear I
> must give you an exact account of the road which led to it; – or to drop
> my metaphor, (for there is nothing more dishonest in an historian
> than the use of one,) – in order to conceive the probability of this error
> in my Uncle Toby aright, I must give you some account of an
> adventure of Trim's, though much against my will. I say much against
> my will, only because the story, in one sense, is certainly out of its
> place here; for by right it should come in, either among the anecdotes
> of my uncle Toby's amours with widow Wadman, in which Corporal
> Trim was no mean actor, – or else in the middle of his and my uncle
> Toby's campaigns on the bowling-green, – for it will do very well in
> either place; – but then if I reserve it for either of those parts of my
> story, – I ruin the story I'm upon; – and if I tell it here – I anticipate

matters, and ruin it there. – What would your worships have me to do in this case? – Tell it, Mr. Shandy, by all means. – You are a fool, Tristram, if you do.

O ye POWERS! (for powers ye are, and great ones too) – which enable mortal man to tell a story worth the hearing – that kindly shew him, where he is to begin it – and where he is to end it – what he is to put into it – and what he is to leave out – how much of it he is to cast into the shade, – and whereabouts he is to throw his light! – Ye, who preside over this vast empire of biographical freebooters, and see how many scrapes and plunges your subjects hourly fall into; – will you do one thing?

I beg and beseech you (in case you will do nothing better for us) that wherever in any part of your dominions it so falls out, that three several roads meet in one point, as they have done just here – that at least you set up a guide-post in the centre of them, in mere charity to direct an uncertain devil which of the three he is to take.

Some of the flavour of *Tristram Shandy* can be found here. There is a direct sense of dialogue between the writer and reader, represented here by the members of Sterne's imaginary readership who offer him advice or raise objections to his procedures. The narrator can even abandon the narrative to offer a prayer to the gods of fiction, asking for their help in the management of his tale. (There may even be a sly reference to the tragic hero, Oedipus, the crisis of whose life began when he found himself at a point where three roads met.) The narrator (perhaps we should stop naïvely confusing Tristram Shandy with Sterne) can take a moment to decide what language is most appropriate to his tale. When he asks if metaphors are suitable to a history, he is raising in a humorous way questions about the nature of prose which had been seriously debated during the seventeenth century. But despite the novel's air of improvisation, we are equally aware that the narrator's stance is not to be taken at face value. Like the professional tight-rope walker, Sterne is highly skilled in the art of fumbling. Elsewhere he makes it plain that everything is planned. Sterne (for it is impossible to believe that Tristram Shandy has *nothing* in common with his author) assures us that his book is so constructed that the digressions form part of the unity of the whole. As he says,

the machinery of my work is of a species by itself; two contrary motions are introduced into it, and reconciled, which were thought to be at variance with each other. In a word, my work is digressive, and it is progressive too – and at the same time.

Although the novel is called *The Life and Opinions of Tristram Shandy*, we hear little of Tristram's life. Sterne begins his story on the night of

Tristram's conception; he does not get born until Volume IV and it is not until Volume VI that he gets his first pair of trousers. The accident to his nose leads to the long digression on noses, and it is followed by the accidental mis-naming of the child. His father wanted to compensate for his lost nose by calling him Trismegistus (the Greek name for the Egyptian god of wisdom, Thoth) but the child was called Tristram instead (in his father's eyes an unfortunate name). After a painful accident with a window-sash, young Tristram disappears from the novel, which ends with an account of Uncle Toby's abortive wooing of widow Wadman.

What keeps this book together is the interplay between the narrator and the reader. Its special fascination is the rich personality which Sterne has given to the voice of the narrator. This 'narrative voice' has a quick-witted knowingness which attracts the reader by its offer of shared confidences; it is indiscreet, arch, occasionally 'naughty'. Such a mannered style may repel many readers, though others will be pleased to recognise the familiar note of a humour that has come to be called 'camp'. It is highly self-conscious and artificial; its indiscreet confidentiality is subject to a strict sense of style, even its indecency is decorous. Contrasted with the narrator are the characters of Walter Shandy and his brother Toby, the first an uncontrolled enthusiast for ideas, explosively outspoken and blunderingly indiscreet, the second, naïvely innocent, transparently good and wholly absorbed by the pure pursuit of military science. Sterne followed the philosopher John Locke (1632–1704) in viewing the mental life as a stream of ideas, linked together by chance, which flowed on beyond the control of the human beings who were its hosts. The Shandy brothers are so bound up in their wholly dissimilar interests that their attention is completely absorbed by their ruling ideas. In Locke's view not only did the mental life run on obsessive tracks, men were also cursed by a physical life which was subject to irrational impulses which had the force of law. To Mr Shandy the body with its pressing needs was an ass. Perhaps the only escape from the absurdity of human life was the withdrawal of the artist to a point of vantage from which he could observe and describe it.

Sterne's literary ancestry goes back to antiquarians like Robert Burton (1577–1640) whose *Anatomy of Melancholy* (1621) is a sprawling assemblage of learned authorities on all the varieties of the moods of men's minds. It may be found in the elaborate verbal humour of Shakespeare's clowns and its mixture of grotesque comedy and sadness. The most obvious source of his kind of literary inventiveness, however, is the sixteenth-century French humanist, François Rabelais (1490–1553) whose fantastic tales of giants, *Gargantua* (1532) and *Pantagruel* (1533), had been vividly translated into English by Sir Thomas Urquhart (1611–60) and published in 1653 and 1693. Rabelais' humour was earthy and excessive, but his extravagant episodes and inexhaustible verbal resourcefulness concealed shrewd satires on contemporary institutions and serious discussion of education, politics and philosophy.

Sterne lacks Rabelais' intellectual toughness, his breadth of humanity and his social awareness. Set beside Rabelais, the seriousness of his art must remain open to question; but his example helped to preserve through the realism and positivism of the nineteenth century a love of paradox, a verbal inventiveness and a scepticism about the value of any conventional formulation of the meaning of life. The short novels of T. L. Peacock (1785–1866) such as *Crotchet Castle* (1831) or *Gryll Grange* (1861) retain something of his heterodox gaiety. Lewis Carroll (pseud. of Charles Lutwidge Dodgson, 1832–98) in *Alice's Adventures in Wonderland* (1865) and *Through the Looking Glass* (1872) shows a comparable love of paradox and a delight in the formal patterns of fiction. But it was not until the twentieth century that Sterne was recognised as a model for the self-conscious novelist, fully aware of the artificiality of his form, unwilling to pretend that he is engaged in anything other than an intricate and elaborate game with his readers. Samuel Beckett (*b.*1906) is such a novelist, especially in his early novels *Murphy* (1938) and *Watt* (1953). So is the Russian writer Vladimir Nabokov (1899–1977) who wrote both in Russian and in English, his adopted language (*Lolita*, 1955; *Pale Fire*, 1962). This elaborately artificial style, under the influence of surrealism, has become international and readers in English have become familiar with the teasing, and often very funny, fantasies of the Argentinian writer J. L. Borges (*b.*1899), the French writer, Raymond Queneau (1903–76) and the Italian Italo Calvino (*b.*1923). Kurt Vonnegut (*b.*1922), Joseph Heller (*b.*1923), John Barth (*b.*1931) and Thomas Pynchon (*b.*1937) are notable American writers of this type and, in *The French Lieutenant's Woman* (1969), John Fowles (*b.*1926) not only introduces the novelist in the character of the rather solemn observant bystander but supplies the novel with alternative endings which are consistent with the development of the plot. Its self-conscious resourcefulness offers a striking example of the contemporary novelist's preoccupation with technique by offering a pastiche of the Victorian novel written from a modern point of view.

Chapter 3

Themes

Introduction

After the foundations of the English novel were laid in the eighteenth century there was a pause in its development. It did not then have its present level of social acceptance, being regarded as lightweight reading material for women or for the less well-educated. In the years of the French Revolution and the Napoleonic Wars, poetry rather than the novel had a predominant place in literature, though some writers such as Robert Bage (1728–1801), Thomas Holcroft (1745–1809) and William Godwin (1756–1836) used the novel interestingly as a means of exploring ideas about the organisation of society. Nevertheless, the novel was on the edge of its greatest period of achievement both in quality and quantity: in 1814 Sir Walter Scott's *Waverley* appeared and two years later John Murray, the publisher of Lord Byron (1788–1824), took over the publication of Jane Austen's *Mansfield Park*. In the early years of the nineteenth century novels were usually published in three volumes (which had some influence on their structure) but changes in the methods of publication, including the serialisation of novels in monthly parts and in magazines, while affecting the structure of the novel also extended its readership, and it is from the 1830s that its predominance must be traced. Its continuing vitality as a form is obvious in the novels which are currently being written by such writers as Anthony Powell (*b.*1905), Angus Wilson (*b.*1913), Anthony Burgess (*b.*1917), Doris Lessing (*b.*1919), Iris Murdoch (*b.*1919) and many others. It has established itself as the leading form of literature all over the English-speaking world – in America, Australia, India, in the Caribbean and in Africa. It would clearly be impossible to offer a history of the form from the time of Scott and Jane Austen to the present. What can usefully be done is to look at some of the predominant themes which novelists have tackled over more than a century and a half of the life of the form. Such an approach will throw light on changes of subject matter and treatment as well as on changes in the forms of fiction itself.

One note of caution should perhaps be sounded. There is some danger in reducing the scope and complexity of a work of art by looking at it in relation to others or in the light of themes they have in common. Novels, plays and poems resemble human beings in their singularity: they cannot be reduced to a common denominator. The material which provides the germ for a novel must first be matured in the imagination of the novelist: in undergoing this process, it develops characteristics which have more to do with the qualities of his vision than with the circumstances of its origin. The proper object of our study must remain the unique character of the individual text. In Chapter 4, special attention will be devoted to what gives particular works their characteristic stamp.

Here we shall concentrate on some of the main topics which have engaged the interest of novelists during the period under review. To some extent the divisions offered are arbitrary and they obviously overlap. There is no reason to suggest that a novel need only have one theme: some novels might easily be mentioned under a number of the headings listed below. The following short list of possible themes is offered as a convenient way of considering some of the major novels and novelists of the period:

   (i) the hero in the making
  (ii) the young woman facing her destiny
 (iii) love and marriage
 (iv) the family
  (v) society
 (vi) politics
 (vii) Utopias (and Dystopias)
(viii) inner worlds
 (ix) adventures

Even such a reduced list of topics cannot be dealt with in full: in the sections that follow some of these themes will be discussed in detail; others will be glanced at but enough will be said to enable interested readers to explore them more fully on their own.

The hero in the making

Henry Fielding's second novel, *Tom Jones* (1749), offers a convenient bridge between the eighteenth and the nineteenth century. It lays down a matrix for a kind of novel which has had a perennial appeal; it deals with the theme of how a young man comes into his inheritance, learns what place he has to occupy in society and what kind of man he is. Born a bastard, brought up by Squire Allworthy, a local philanthropist, Tom does not learn until the end of the novel that he is in truth the Squire's nephew. Only then does he demonstrate that he is fit for the position his birth has entitled him to. The foundling becomes a gentleman; the prodigal returns to the deserved affection of the man who has brought him up. He also gains the love of the good and beautiful woman whom he has almost alienated by his behaviour. *Tom Jones* is partly parable, partly fairy-tale. It is also a long and complex sequence of episodes the ramifications of which are so expertly managed by Fielding that the reader's attention is held in suspense until the last chapter.

One striking aspect of the theme of the hero in the making, as handled by Fielding, is its relative modesty. In later novels, we might be surprised to find any limit being placed on the ambition of a young man who was making his way in the world. The phenomenon of Napoleon's early career perhaps suggested that illimitable vistas were open to the young man who wished to carve out a place for himself in society. The French novelists Stendhal (pseud. of Henri Beyle, 1783–1842) and Balzac (1799–1850) loved to describe the efforts of heroes who tried to make their way from humble beginnings to wealth, influence and power over beautiful women. Fielding works within narrower constraints. Society for him is stratified and much less vulnerable to assault, even if such social climbing were desirable. The action of *Tom Jones* takes place at the time of the second Jacobite Rebellion in 1745 and in the main inset story in the novel, a long personal narrative told by the misanthropic Man of the Hill (Bk.8, 11–14), reference is made to the unsuccessful revolt of the Duke of Monmouth (1649–85) and to the unconstitutional role of James II (1633–1701). Fielding dislikes Jacobitism and rebellious behaviour; he certainly does not encourage young men to get on by attacking the foundations of society.

The action of the novel takes place along a geographical line between London and Squire Allworthy's home in the West Country. With some qualifications, town and country have for Fielding the traditional connotations of good and evil. Cast out by his misdemeanours from his uncle's favour, Tom makes his way to London followed by his sweetheart, Sophia Western, whose father wants her to marry Allworthy's legitimate nephew, Blifil, an unsavoury self-seeker. From Somerset to London is a journey from innocence to experience, from untried, rather careless goodness to a tempered knowledge of the dangers of temptation. By the end of the novel Tom knows the frailty of human intentions and has learnt respect for the moderate virtue of prudence.

Tom's testing takes place at the hands of Lady Bellaston, a middle-aged but still susceptible London society woman to whose wiles he falls victim and from whom he receives payment for his services. Fielding frankly describes the sexual laxity of the times: high-spirited young men behaved coarsely, especially with women of the lower orders. Fashionable women might fall unsuitably in love with their men-servants.

The first hint that behaviour of this kind might lead to unacceptable degradation comes in the tale of the Man of the Hill which is devoted to showing how gambling, sexual laxity and dishonesty have led the Man of the Hill to a settled loathing of mankind which makes him say

'Human nature is everywhere the same, everywhere the object of detestation and avoidance.' Tom does not share this pessimism but during his stay in London he skirts the edge of the moral abyss the Man of the Hill experienced. Since this is a comedy, the vice, murder and even incest which successively threaten to destroy Tom's character are little more than passing scares, but Fielding so involves Tom in disgrace that there is real risk that the ties of affection that have linked him to Sophia will be permanently weakened. He begins to see the dishonour of being a kept man. In seeing how his friend Nightingale behaves towards the woman he has seduced and plans to abandon, he redefines for himself the principles of honourable behaviour between the sexes. The return to domestic happiness and rural tranquillity is not for Tom the ignominious retreat that a similar return to the country will be for the hero of Flaubert's *Education Sentimentale* (1869). For Fielding, domestic happiness in a well-ordered kingdom is the best state of life a man can hope for.

Tom Jones was set in the time of the second Jacobite rebellion: the action of Walter Scott's *Waverley* also takes place during that rebellion. Its subtitle, 'Tis Sixty Years Since, measures the distance between Fielding's contemporary view and Scott's appraisal of events that have become history. Young Edward Waverley, Scott's hero in the making, undergoes a political rather than a strictly ethical education, though these concepts cannot be entirely separated. What is at stake in *Waverley* is not the morality of sex but the morality of citizenship. In both novels 'honour' is a key-word: in *Tom Jones* it is a concept which orders the relationship between men and women; in *Waverley* it orders the relationship between the individual and the state.

Edward Waverley is the son of a man who has abandoned the traditional loyalty of his ancestors to serve the newly established Hanoverian King George II, but Waverley himself has been brought up as heir to his Jacobite uncle. He joins the Royal army to satisfy his father's wishes and finds himself in Scotland where he is brought in contact first with an old Jacobite friend of his uncle's and then with a more dubious Highland Chieftain, Fergus MacIvor, who is in secret correspondence with the Stuart Pretender in France. He falls in love first with Rose Bradwardine, daughter of his uncle's old friend, and then with Flora MacIvor, sister of Fergus. Both these girls stand as symbols of different aspects of the old cause. Swept into the rebel camp, Waverley finds himself involved in the march south in support of Charles Edward Stuart, the Young Pretender. The servant who has followed him from his uncle's estate dies before his eyes and he sees the colonel of the regiment in which he served cut down in battle. All of these events occur in a cause for which he can find little rational justification. As he puts it to himself, before chance involves him on the rebel's side:

Whatever were the original rights of the Stuarts, calm reflection told him, that, omitting the question how far James the Second could forfeit those of his posterity, he had, according to the united voice of the whole nation, justly forfeited his own. Since that period, four monarchs had reigned in peace and glory over Britain, sustaining and exalting the character of the nation abroad, and its liberties at home. Reason asked, was it worthwhile to disturb a government so long settled and established, and to plunge a kingdom into all the miseries of civil war, for the purpose of replacing upon the throne the descendants of a monarch by whom it had been wilfully forfeited?

These ancient quarrels may seem remote, but the issues Scott deals with are fresh and lively today. Fergus MacIvor and his beautiful sister are fanatical adherents of their own cause for which nothing is too precious to be sacrificed. Though reportedly 'wedded to honour', Fergus turns out to be keenly interested in the earldom which he stands to gain from a Jacobite victory. It is Flora who represents pure devotion to principle. Scott suggests, as Shakespeare did in his history plays, the fearful waste of civil war. Two scenes in particular carry this message: the first is the scene of destruction at the castle of Baron Bradwardine when Waverley visits it after the rebellion is over. He had first come there when he arrived in Scotland and approached it along a woodland path which led to the main gates of the castle. It is lovingly and minutely described by Scott, and Edward is impressed by the ancient beauty of the scene. On his return he approaches by the same path.

A single glance announced that great changes had taken place. One half of the gate, entirely destroyed and split up for firewood, lay in piles ready to be taken away; the other swung uselessly upon its loosened hinges. The battlements above the gate were broken and thrown down, and the carved bears, which were said to have done sentinel's duty upon the top for centuries, now, hurled from their posts, lay among the rubbish. The avenue was cruelly wasted. Several large trees were felled and left lying across the path; and the cattle of the villagers, and the more rude hoofs of dragoon horses, had poached into black mud the verdant turf which Waverley had so admired.

The personal consequences of the rebellion are grimmer still. As Waverley leaves the town of Carlisle after keeping vigil with Fergus during the last night before the latter's execution for treason, he checks a glance back at the battlements of the town gate. But, as one of his Scottish servants says,

'They're no there . . . the heads are ower the Scotch gate, as they ca' it. It's a great pity of Evan Dhu [Fergus's loyal clansman] who was a very weel-meaning good-natured man, to be a Hieland man; and indeed so was the Laird o' Glennaquoich [Fergus] too, for that matter, when he wasna in ane o' his tirrivies [rages].'

This disparaging note concludes the story of the romantic adventure which ended in death, destruction and the cruel but necessary vengeance of the law. Waverley has broken with Flora, and will marry Rose Bradwardine, gentle, peace-loving and domesticated. Scott's heroes are not noted for the robustness of their personality: Edward Waverley is a pair of eyes through which Scott's view of the condition of Britain at a certain moment in its history is presented. But the emphasis is on the maturing of Waverley's political understanding. Despite Scott's occasional prolixity, *Waverley* is a keenly felt and movingly expressed novel which invites comparison with Standhal's *Charterhouse of Parma* (1839).

Later heroes of English fiction are thoroughly domesticated. Charles Dickens (1812–70) and W. M. Thackeray (1811–63) both wrote novels about a young man's entry into society which are largely autobiographical. But by the 1840s a distinct change had come over the manners of English society. The vigour and frankness of Fielding could no longer be tolerated. In *Pendennis* (1849) Thackeray attempted to paint a portrait of one of 'the gentlemen of our age' but he offered this warning to his readers:

> Since the author of *Tom Jones* was buried, no writer of fiction among us has been permitted to depict to his utmost power a MAN. We must drape him and give him a certain conventional simper. Society will not tolerate the natural in our Art. Many ladies have remonstrated and subscribers left me because, in the course of the story, I described a young man resisting and affected by temptation. My object was to say that he had the passions to feel, and the manliness and generosity to overcome them. You will not hear – it is best to know it – what moves in the real world, what passes in society, in the clubs, colleges, mess-rooms, – what is the life and talk of your sons.

The growing reticence and social repressiveness which cast some shadow over the high spirits of Jane Austen's novels had deep effects on English society and on the art which reflected it. The evasion of truth which Thackeray deplores first affected, and then became the subject-matter of, the English novel. Novelists who wished to expose the hypocrisy of the public silence on sexual behaviour in particular had to find ways of referring to matters which could not be discussed explicitly. Much of the history of the novel in modern times has been concerned with the breaking of these taboos.

Thackeray's *Pendennis* and Dickens's *David Copperfield* ran together as serials in 1849. They both told the story of a young man's education, his entry into the world, his love affairs, his attempts at finding employment before he finds success as an author, and his marriage (or marriages). These novels provide fascinating glimpses into interestingly different areas of English life: their presentation is also strikingly different. *Pendennis* in particular is touched with nostalgia and a chagrined sense of the narrowness of life. Superficially, Arthur Pendennis, the hero of the novel, achieves success and a good marriage. After squandering his money and wasting his time at Oxford, he starts a literary career in London. He narrowly misses entering into a loveless marriage with the high-spirited but selfish Blanche Amory and ends by marrying the girl his mother always intended for him, who has been his friend since childhood. *Pendennis* is very far from being as thinly sentimental as this drastic reduction of its plot makes it appear. The novel is loosely organised around the callous and very often hilariously funny youthful adventures of Pendennis, but it is primarily about English – and especially, London – life and its characters. Despite its liveliness and brilliant description of the London scene, there is an undercurrent of pessimistic acceptance in *Pendennis*: the world is as it is fated to be. Thackeray does not have Fielding's astringent sense of what makes for decent behaviour. Instead of the picture of MAN which he feared the age would not accept, he has given us a picture of Arthur Pendennis, the ordinary well-meaning chap who goes through life as best he can and has some luck in the end. Running through the novel is a sense that men are not masters of their fate: Thackeray is sharply and sadly aware of the settled, limited, mechanical life of the mature man pushing its way through the playfulness, the gaucheness or the idealism of the young man. He ends his novel with the following words:

> If the best men do not draw the great prizes in life, we know it has been so settled by the Ordainer of the lottery. We own, and see daily, how the false and worthless live and prosper, while the good are called away, and the dear and young perish untimely – we perceive in every man's life the maimed happiness, the frequent falling, the bootless endeavour, the struggle of Right and Wrong, in which the strong often succumb and the swift fail: we see the flowers of good blowing in foul places, as, in the most lofty and splendid fortunes, flaws of vice and meanness, and stains of evil; and knowing how mean the best of us is, let us give a hand of charity to Arthur Pendennis, with all his faults and shortcomings, who does not claim to be a hero, but only a man and a brother.

Thackeray had an immense admiration for Fielding, but, compared to the earlier writer, he speaks in tones of chastened experience. In

Thackeray's novels, men face the surprises and disappointments of life: women are either too fragile to bear such knowledge or they have their own deeper intuition which provides solace, if not enlightenment, about life's meaning and purpose.

The title of Thackeray's novel is *The History of Pendennis*; the full title of Dickens's novel, as it appeared in the first number, was *The Personal History, Adventures, Experience and Observations of David Copperfield, the Younger*. The word 'personal' marks a significant difference of emphasis. *David Copperfield* is written in the first person rather than the third and the tone of the narrative is quite different from that of *Pendennis*. Whereas the narrator of *Pendennis* is looking with a worldly-wise amusement on the young man whose history he is relating, the narrator in *David Copperfield* is David himself. His narration, especially of his childhood, has a quality of instant recall, of active contemporaneous participation which we have come to associate with the vivid remembrance of early experience in some of the poetry of William Wordsworth (1770–1850) or with Marcel Proust's (1871–1922) long novel *A la recherche du temps perdu* (1913–27). Here is David's description of the superannuated boat in which his mother's servant's brother, Mr Peggotty, lives at Yarmouth.

It was beautifully clean inside, and as tidy as possible. There was a table, and a Dutch clock, and a chest of drawers, and on the chest of drawers there was a tea-tray with a painting on it of a lady with a parasol, taking a walk with a military-looking child who was trundling a hoop. The tray was kept from tumbling down, by a bible; and the tray, if it had tumbled down, would have smashed a quantity of cups and saucers and a teapot that were grouped around the book. On the walls there were some common coloured pictures, framed and glazed, of scripture subjects; such as I have never seen since in the hands of pedlars, without seeing the whole interior of Peggotty's brother's house again, at one view. Abraham in red going to sacrifice Isaac in blue, and Daniel in yellow cast into a den of green lions, were the most prominent of these. Over the little mantel-shelf, was a picture of the Sarah Jane lugger, built at Sunderland, with a real little wooden stern stuck on to it; a work of art, combining composition with carpentry, which I considered to be one of the most enviable possessions that the world could afford . . . .

All this I saw in the first glance as I crossed the threshold . . . and then Peggotty opened a little door and showed me my bedroom. It was the completest and most desirable bedroom ever seen – in the stern of the vessel; with a little window, where the rudder used to go through; a little looking-glass, just the right height for me, nailed against the wall, and framed with oyster-shells; a little bed, which there was just enough room to get into; and a nosegay of seaweed in a blue mug on the table. The walls were whitewashed as white as milk, and the patchwork counterpane made my eyes quite ache with its brightness. One thing I particularly noticed in this delightful house was the smell of fish; which was so searching that when I took out my pocket-handkerchief to wipe my nose, I found it smelt exactly as if it had wrapped up a lobster. On my imparting this discovery in confidence to Peggotty, she informed me that her brother dealt in lobsters, crabs, and crawfish; and I afterwards found that a heap of these creatures, in a state of wonderful conglomeration with one another, and never leaving off pinching whatever they laid hold of, were usually to be found in a little wooden outhouse where the pots and kettles were kept.

Readers may like to consider what they make of this extract from the novel: it is clearly very different from the reminiscences of Defoe's Colonel Jack. Some of the detail of this passage may appear quaintly sentimental. It is stamped with the personal: what David remembers is less important than the fact that David remembers it. Perhaps there is something cosily self-regarding about this act of memory, but on the other hand it is the memory of a child, and perhaps has some of that inability to distinguish between self and not-self which modern psychologists have described as a mark of the immaturity of children. Some of the objects remembered have a more functional significance, because they relate to larger themes in the novel. Abraham and Isaac remind us of the theme of the sacrifice of the innocent, the willingness of fathers to offer up their sons, which is exemplified in the relationship between David and his stepfather, Mr Murdstone, or between David and Mr Creakle, the proprietor of David's first school. In the same way, like Daniel in the lion's den, David is often at bay among his enemies.

Whatever reservations we may have about the way this passage is written, a careful re-reading leaves us with the strong impression that this view of Peggotty's house has the clear-eyed innocence of childhood. Perhaps only the heap of lobsters, wonderfully conglomerated, has the objectification of things seen for their own sake which suggests the wholly disinterested vision. But the reader will have to make his or her own judgment: is there, for example, in the first part of the description a touch of condescension? It is, of course, part of David's character that he fails to appreciate the values of the Peggotty household until it is too late, so the mixed impression which this passage gives – condescension, egotistic self-regard and a capacity for the clear-eyed apprehension of the truth – is appropriate to the mixture of wisdom and weakness which David displays during the course of the novel.

David Copperfield is a novel about the personal life: through it Dickens announces the value of individual experience, the right of human beings to privacy, personal freedom, the happy satisfaction of private interests and the possibility of mature relationships with others. These are not won without difficulty, and, as the examples of Emily and Martha Endell show, there is a special difficulty for women whose 'freedom' seems entirely dependent upon men. *David Copperfield* describes David's achievement of maturity, but it is also concerned with the theme of marriage. David has some of the characteristics of Tom Jones: his period of apprenticeship is devoted to preparing him for a life of domestic happiness. Fielding does not discuss the question of how this happiness is to be achieved: Sophia's beauty and virtue are sufficient guarantees of a successful marriage. Dickens is aware of human complexities which go beyond this simple view. David's first marriage to Dora Spenlow is unhappy because it is not a marriage of minds and purposes.

David Copperfield is studded with unhappy personal relationships, with bad marriages and inadequate fathers. His mother's second marriage to Mr Murdstone was disastrous; his aunt Betsey Trotwood married a man who spent her fortune, broke her heart and became a bigamist, an adventurer, a gambler and a cheat. Dr Strong, the unworldly master of David's second school, finds that his marriage to a much younger woman has been manipulated by her relatives to their own mercenary ends; the marriage of Mr and Mrs Micawber is a tragi-comic match between slovenliness and improvidence; even Traddles, whose wife is devoted to him, has to cope with the demands of her extensive family.

If Dickens felt the pressure of the conventions of repression which we have come to call 'Victorian', he responded to them by developing a language that had a power to suggest what could not be openly stated. The description of Uriah Heep, for example – his damp hand, 'like a frog', his 'shadowless red eyes, which looked as if they had scorched their lashes off . . . the disagreeable dints . . . in his nostrils coming and going with his breath', the 'shaky undulation pervading his frame from his chin to his boots' – acquires nauseating overtones in the context of his aspirations to marry Agnes Wickfield, the daughter of the partner he is systematically defrauding. It is possible to see some of Dickens's melodrama as a legitimate attempt to present in one picture the two sides of Victorian society; Virtue confronting Vice cannot but be a melodramatic tableau. Rosa Dartle's tirade against Emily, back in London after leaving her betrayer, Steerforth, is shrill and rancorous but it does suggest the withering of the imagination which followed the stifling of natural feeling: Martha Endell, the abandoned woman, is an *alter ego* of the unfulfilled spinster. On the whole, however, the reader is bound to be disappointed by Dickens's failure to do justice to the serious themes he advances. David's pain and unhappiness in his marriage to

Dora are expressed but not fully explored: conveniently falling into a decline, she dies and leaves the way clear for Agnes Wickfield, who has always been David's true love.

Another of Dickens's finest novels, *Great Expectations* (1860-1) deals with the theme of the young man's initiation into society. Dickens was aware that he was working with material he had already used in *David Copperfield* but the two novels are very different. *Great Expectations* combines the story of the maturing of its central character, Pip, with a considered critique of the society to which he belongs. *Great Expectations* is a more carefully composed novel than *David Copperfield*; the methods of symbolism and poetic suggestion which Dickens used in the earlier novel are more fully developed here. Wemmick, Mr Jagger, Miss Havisham and Magwitch, the convict who becomes Pip's benefactor, are conceived as living representatives of forces in society which restrict and distort the growth of human personality. Pip's capacity for love is demonstrated in the course of the novel as he begins to come to terms with the disreputable source of his worldly advancement. Pip's own sense of guilt and his understanding of his egotism and snobbery are clearly and painfully made evident. On the advice of a friend, Dickens softened the original ending of the novel in which he was content to reward his hero with nothing more than moral enlightenment. As it stands now, the reconciliation with Estella, the girl he loved, who has been trained to torment the men who fall in love with her, has a fine sobriety. Pip and Estella's frank recognition of each other's frailties has the kind of honesty which *David Copperfield* lacks.

If Dickens's novels reach out beyond immediate impressions of the particular experiences of everyday life to a wider consideration of the structure of society, the movement of the novel during the rest of the century was towards the faithful delineation of private experience. It might be said that the task set for the novelist in the later years of the Victorian period was to remove the drapes of convention from the male and female figures that appeared in their work. The moral hero of modern fiction is the man (or woman) who looks at life with unblinkered honesty. Part of this honesty was an open acknowledgment of the power of money and of sex in human affairs. Although Victorian novels talk much of love and marriage, they say less about sexual attraction. Towards the end of the century the strain of this repressiveness was beginning to be felt. One interesting novel which dealt with the force of adolescent feeling (as contrasted with adult calculation) is *The Ordeal of Richard Feverel* (1859) by George Meredith (1828-1909). For some readers this novel (and other novels by the same author) will appear fatally flawed by a prose style which is more witty, ornate and artificial than its subject matter can bear. It deals with the education and growth to manhood of a boy whose father believes he has perfected a system of education which will mould the young man's will to his own lofty but essentially worldly aims. These hopes do not survive Richard's first experience of genuine sexual passion: the outcome for the young people is tragedy, but the chapters in which young Richard meets the girl with whom he falls in love are written with a lyricism and romantic ardour which point forward to the early work of D. H. Lawrence (1885–1930).

Three novels bring us from Victorianism to modernism: *Jude the Obscure* (1895) by Thomas Hardy (1840–1928), *Sons and Lovers* (1913) by D. H. Lawrence and *A Portrait of the Artist as a Young Man* (1916) by James Joyce (1882–1941). Perhaps Hardy's novel is better described as the unmaking of a hero, since the story of Jude is a record of tragic failure. In this novel Hardy has pitted his hero against all the negative elements of Victorian society. The sensitive poor man who was keen on learning had little chance of a conventional formal education in a society where this was the prerogative of a close-knit caste. Jude's Christminster might be compared with Pendennis's Oxbridge. St Boniface's College is a place where Pendennis will drink, gamble and make friends with the right people; but for Jude, Biblioll College offers a dream of learning which he is never to realise. To the stone-mason's request for advice on how to enter, its Master replies, 'I venture to think that you will have a much better chance of life by remaining in your own sphere and sticking to your trade than by adopting any other course.' Unfortunately, the advice is sound. Jude's attempt to 'better' himself fails in the face of centuries of accumulated class prejudice and of the impossibility of reconciling the aspirations of his mind and soul with the 'impulses – affections – vices perhaps they should be called' of his body. As he says bitterly outside the gates of 'the circular theatre . . . which stood in his mind as the sad symbol of his abandoned hopes' (the Sheldonian Theatre in Oxford), he would have had to be 'as cold-blooded as a fish and as selfish as a pig to have a really good chance of being one of his country's worthies'. Without money or position, the satisfaction of one set of aspirations involved the rigid denial of the other.

The women in Jude's life extend and complicate the picture of the constant warfare between soul and body which Hardy offers in his characterisation of Jude. Arabella, his first wife, captures him with a frank offer of sensual pleasure; Sue Bridehead, the cousin he loves, is more akin to him intellectually and spiritually, but she too is torn between hedonistic emancipation and religious beliefs which urge renunciation and asceticism. The underlying theme which unites the separate struggles of Jude and Sue for freedom and personal dignity is the appalling weight of the dead hand of custom. The forces of repression are institutionalised in a class-system which is supported by the powerful authority of religion and scholarship; no less powerful are the internal mechanisms of conscience which are unconsciously modelled on the external forces which impose order on society. Conscious human effort, Hardy suggests, is no match for this alliance between society and super-ego.

As Hardy puts it in the preface to the first edition of the novel, *Jude the Obscure* was 'addressed by a man to men and women of full age; [it attempted] to deal unaffectedly with the fret and fever, derision and disaster, that may press in the wake of the strongest passion known to humanity; to tell, without a mincing of words, of a deadly war waged between flesh and spirit; and to point the tragedy of unfulfilled aims'. Lawrence and Joyce made very much greater demands on the tolerance and maturity of their readership and extended Hardy's exploration of the dynamics of human psychology. They did not share his pessimism about the range of human freedom: in his early novels, at least, Lawrence expresses the exhilaration of sense experience: looking, touching and feeling are primary sources of satisfaction which persist no matter what frustrations the will may suffer. Here is Mrs Morel, the mother of the central figure of *Sons and Lovers*, Paul Morel, taking her baby son out on an evening stroll:

She went over the sheep-bridge and across the corner of the meadow to the cricket-ground. The meadows seemed one space of ripe, evening light, whispering with the distant mill-race. She sat on a seat under the alders in the cricket-ground, and fronted the evening. Before her, level and solid, spread the big green cricket-field, like the bed of a sea of light. Children played in the bluish shadow of the pavilion. Many rooks, high up, came cawing home across the softly-woven sky. They stooped in a long curve down into the golden glow, concentrating, cawing, wheeling, like black flakes on a slow vortex, over a tree-clump that made a dark boss among the pasture . . . .

The sun was going down. Every open evening, the hills of Derbyshire were blazed over with red sunset. Mrs. Morel watched the sun sink from the glistening sky, leaving a soft flower-blue overhead, while the western space went red, as if all the fire had swum down there, leaving the bell cast flawless blue. The mountain-ash berries across the field stood fierily out from the dark leaves, for a moment. A few shocks of corn in a corner of the fallow stood up as if alive; she imagined them bowing; perhaps her son would be a Joseph. In the east, a mirrored sunset floated pink opposite the west's scarlet. The big haystacks on the hillside, that butted into the glare, went cold . . . .

In her arms lay the delicate baby. Its deep blue eyes, always looking up at her unblinking, seemed to draw her innermost thoughts out of her. She no longer loved her husband; she had not wanted this child to come, and there it lay in her arms and pulled at her heart. She felt as if the navel string that had connected its frail little body with hers had not been broken. A wave of hot love went over her to the infant. She held it close to her face and breast. With all her force, with all her soul she would make up to it for having brought it into the world unloved. She would love it all the more now it was here; carry it in her love. Its clear, knowing eyes gave her pain and fear. Did it know all about her? When it lay under her heart, had it been listening then? Was there a reproach in the look? She felt the marrow melt in her bones, with fear and pain.

In the final paragraph of this extract the central theme of the novel – the intense relationship between mother and son – is stated. Thackeray in *Pendennis*, had talked of the 'sexual jealousy' Pen's mother had for her son's girl-friends, but he had not dealt in detail with these matters. What is more striking, perhaps, about Lawrence's approach is its matching of seeing and understanding. For Mrs Morel, 'it was one of these still moments when the small frets vanish, and the beauty of things stands out, and she had the peace and the strength to see herself'. Such a way of putting it takes us straight back to Wordsworth's 'Tintern Abbey' (1798) in which he speaks of

> that blessed mood,
> In which the burthen of the mystery,
> In which the heavy and the weary weight
> Of all this unintelligible world,
> Is lightened: – that serene and blessed mood,
> In which the affections gently lead us on, –
> Until, the breath of this corporeal frame
> And even the motion of our human blood
> Almost suspended, we are laid asleep
> In body, and become a living soul:
> While with an eye made quiet by the power
> Of harmony, and the deep power of joy,
> We see into the life of things.

Something of this spiritual tranquillity and refined joy has been induced in Mrs Morel by her contemplation of the physical scene around her. Notice how Lawrence evokes ideas of unity and harmony: 'the meadows . . . whispering with the distant mill-race;' the birds swirling downwards in a vortex that has for its centre the clump of trees; the symmetry of the mirror image of the western sunset in the eastern sky and the dome of blue which surmounts the whole scene. In the symbolism of Lawrence's language, flowers stand for achieved individual wholeness. Mrs Morel foresees power for her son, but she also sees him as a truth-teller, someone who will penetrate the secret meaning of her own life, and this vision inspires her with fear. It would be interesting to compare Lawrence's language with Meredith's in *The Ordeal of Richard Feverel*. Meredith constantly runs the risk of being 'poetical' in quite the wrong sense – elaborate, lush, flashy, over-ambitious – at worst, meretricious. Lawrence has done what we may assume Meredith tried to do: he has absorbed into his prose the finest elements of English Romantic poetry, which at its best saw the real world as a physical manifestation of the ideal and expressed its vision in essentially simple language.

Sons and Lovers, like *Pendennis*, *David Copperfield* and *A Portrait of the Artist as a Young Man*, is autobiographical. *Sons and Lovers*, however, is focused upon Paul Morel's psychological development. In the background of the novel is the pain of his mother's unfulfilled life which ends with the physical pain of cancer: Mrs Morel tries to find in her sons the fulfilment she has failed to find in her husband. The eldest dies; Paul has to fight her to find his own life. He has also to fight with Miriam who has some of the qualities and some of the defects of Hardy's Sue Bridehead. Once again, however, Lawrence presents Miriam more successfully because of his extraordinary sense of detail, his knack of finding incidents which express what his characters are feeling. What Lawrence brought to the novel was a power of psychological analysis which was quite new. Where Dickens suggested depth of feeling under the surface of appearances, Lawrence goes directly to the most sensitive feelings which are constantly in play beneath the ordinary movements of everyday life.

A Portrait of the Artist as a Young Man is one of the greatest of modern novels. It traces in a wholly impersonal way the development of a boy into the writer he is destined to be. Joyce arranged his novel in five chapters which trace Stephen Dedalus's life from boyhood to young manhood. The boy's fascination with language indicates his calling, and the language of the novel extends in complexity in sympathy with the development of Stephen's own powers. He moves from the innocence of childhood to frenzied episodes of adolescent lust and then to a calm contemplation of women as a source of literary inspiration. His family and schoolmasters want him to become a priest and he is destined to become a priest of the imagination: he resists temptations to a life of action in favour of the dedicated celebration of common life which is his true life's work. Joyce links the sections of his novel – and the phases of Stephen's life – with elaborate patterns of symbols which echo and re-echo through the text. Women in many guises – sweethearts, casually encountered country women, street-walkers, women in books he has read, the Blessed Virgin – represent in incomplete form the perfect image of the Muse who guides his imagination. Bogs, stagnant water, muddy pools represent the Ireland from which he wants to escape; streams, flowing rivers, tides of the sea represent the currents which pull him towards his vocation as an artist. In his university friends he sees images of himself as he might be if he remained in Ireland. A central metaphor which pervades the novel is his name: Stephen Dedalus, part martyr, part pioneer and hero, poet and maker, risking everything to reach new heights of artistic endeavour; saving his own life and art by 'silence, exile and cunning'.

The young woman facing her destiny

'... the conception of a certain young woman affronting her destiny, had begun with being all my outfit for the large building of *The Portrait of a Lady*', says Henry James (1843–1916). Isabel Archer – the young woman in question – faced a destiny of singular bleakness; having married a worthless man, she chose to persist in her marriage rather than accept the love offered to her by another man. In his Preface to the novel, James speaks of the uncommonness of selecting a woman for the central figure of a work of fiction. Women, James thinks, have been thought of as too frail to support this role; generally speaking, they are seen in relation to others. It may certainly seem true that, until recent times, women's destiny was thought to be marriage. Failure to marry was the fate that was most to be feared for women in the novels of the nineteenth century. The inferior status of women was accentuated by their restricted access to education and to employment. Such employment as was open to them was limited and ill-paid. The fear of being a governess, subject to the pleasure of a vulgar or indifferent family, hangs over many of the heroines of nineteenth-century novels; some, like Charlotte Brontë's (1816–55) Jane Eyre or Lucy Snowe (in *Villette*) actually suffer it, and Ursula Brangwen in *The Rainbow* (1915) by D. H. Lawrence endures the grinding work of teaching a primary class of over a hundred pupils.

What is of interest in the novels which treat of women's role in life is therefore not the range of choices open to them; it is very much, however, the variety of expectation and response which they display within it. Marriage offered a decent, if dependent, life but it might be dearly bought. In *Pride and Prejudice* (1813) by Jane Austen, Charlotte Lucas marries the dull, conceited clergyman, William Collins, because she cannot bear to refuse a reasonable offer. As she explains to her friend, Elizabeth Bennett,

'... I am not romantic you know; I never was. I ask only a comfortable home; and considering Mr Collins's character, connections, and situation in life, I am convinced that my chance of happiness with him is as fair, as most people can boast on entering the marriage state'.

Elizabeth quietly answered 'Undoubtedly'; – and after an awkward pause, they returned to the rest of the family. Charlotte did not stay much longer, and Elizabeth was then left to reflect on what she had heard. It was a long time before she became at all reconciled to the idea of so unsuitable a match . . . . She had always felt that Charlotte's opinion of matrimony was not exactly like her own, but she could not have supposed it possible that, when called into action, she would have sacrificed every better feeling to worldly advantage. Charlotte the wife of Mr. Collins, was a most humiliating picture! – And to the pang of a friend disgracing herself and sunk in her esteem, was added the distressing conviction that it was impossible for that friend to be tolerably happy in the lot she had chosen.

It is a sad mistake to see Jane Austen as preoccupied with worldly success and the nice calculation of income and estate. Money was undoubtedly necessary and significant in the lives of Jane Austen's women because it assured a level of privacy, independence and freedom to maintain certain social values which they (and she) thought worth while. For an unmarried woman the line between independence and drudgery was easily crossed. George Eliot (1819–80) makes this point in her characterisation of Mr Tulliver's sister in *Mill on the Floss* (1860); Henry James makes it about Kate Croy in *The Wings of the Dove* (1902) and Jane Austen had made it tellingly in her description of Fanny Price's home in Portsmouth in *Mansfield Park* (1814). In her own life Jane Austen had experienced the precariousness of a woman's independence; her private life of imaginative creativity had to fit in with the demands of a large circle of family and friends. Of the women in her novels perhaps only Emma Woodhouse thought of herself as having a personal independence which she might use as she wished. *Emma* (1816) is Jane Austen's fourth published novel. It is set in 'the large and populous village almost amounting to a town' of Highbury, where Mr Woodhouse has a substantial property. *Emma* is a penetrating story of self-discovery, infinitely sharper in its dissection of the self-deception of its protagonist than *David Copperfield* or *Pendennis*. Marriage may have been the expected outcome for her heroines but Jane Austen is not content to relate a simple story of courtship with its tribulations and ultimate success. In her novels 'love' has clear ethical and spiritual connotations. Her lovers are not expressing any simple domestic affection; they are affirming values upon which their civilised society depends.

Emma is blind about herself, her friends, her own wishes and her own best interests. She takes an interest in Harriet Smith, a girl of no family and uncertain parentage, who has been educated at the local school. Harriet is interested in a decent local farmer but Emma encourages her to set her sights higher. She first tries to throw Harriet into the arms of Mr Elton, a young clergyman who has a rather higher sense of what is due to him. He surprises Emma by proposing to her; when she refuses, he soon returns with an acceptable bride. Emma and Harriet are then involved with Frank Churchill, a neighbour's son who has been adopted as the heir of a rich family; his parents see Emma as a suitable match for him; Emma thinks Harriet might be in love with him; in fact, he is secretly engaged to Jane Fairfax, the niece of a poor and rather ridiculous spinster. Finally, to her horror, Emma discovers that Harriet is really in love with Mr Knightley, a neighbouring landowner and Emma's brother-in-law, who has been her friend for years. Her feelings on hearing this news give her some insight into her own affections.

None of this story would be interesting if Emma Woodhouse was not someone we could care about. By rapid summary and a brilliantly apt choice of where to begin her story, Jane Austen immerses us in the nuances of small-town life in the south of England, early in the nineteenth century. In the following extract all the members of the Woodhouse family now left at home, namely, Emma and her father, receive a visit from Mr Knightley just after the wedding of Miss Taylor, who has been governess and friend to Emma and her sister. Mr Woodhouse speaks first:

'Ah! poor Miss Taylor! 'Tis a sad business.'

'Poor Mr and Miss Woodhouse, if you please; but I cannot possibly say "poor Miss Taylor." I have a great regard for you and Emma; but when it comes to the question of dependence or independence! – At any rate, it must be better to have only one to please, than two.'

'Especially when *one* of those two is such a fanciful, troublesome creature!' said Emma playfully. 'That is what you have in your head, I know – and what you would certainly say if my father were not by.'

'I believe it is very true, my dear, indeed,' said Mr Woodhouse, with a sigh. 'I am afraid I am sometimes very fanciful and troublesome.'

'My dearest papa! You do not think I could mean *you*, or suppose Mr Knightley to mean *you*. What a horrible idea! Oh, no! I meant only myself. Mr Knightley loves to find a fault with me, you know – in a joke – it is all a joke. We always say what we like to one another.'

Mr Knightley, in fact, was one of the few people who could see faults in Emma Woodhouse, and the only one who ever told her of them: and though this was not particularly agreeable to Emma herself, she knew it would be so much less so to her father, that she would not have him really suspect such a circumstance as her not being thought perfect by every body.

The theme of *Emma* is 'dependence or independence' – but of mind rather than of pocket. To understand how Jane Austen handles this

theme we must listen to the voices of her characters – and especially to
the voice of the narrator – with great care. What deduction are we to
draw from the final words of the narrative comment? Is Emma
protecting her father's image of her or is she protecting her own image of
herself? Or has she simply not begun to think about her own character:
is there a real danger that she secretly suspects she *may* be perfect?
Understanding others is difficult, especially if our perceptions are dulled
by prejudice or self-absorption. We are given the word 'playfully' to
hear Emma's tone of voice, but her father, his mind clouded by
imaginary ills, misses it. Emma's witty high spirits run the risk of
insincerity: she is good at the kind of conversation that promises no
commitment. But she is genuinely concerned, as we see here, if her
teasing remarks go astray. She is to learn during the course of the novel
how deeply such talk can hurt.

Mr Knightley is immediately established as a man of discernment,
honesty and candour, interested enough in Emma to take notice of her,
concerned enough to speak genuinely to her. The courtship of Emma
and Mr Knightley – the unavowed mainspring of the novel – is a gradual
matching of styles of speech; 'liveliness' is one thing: insincerity is quite
another. Mr Knightley's grave conversation implies a deep attachment
to values which are gradually revealed by the unfolding action of the
novel.

Emma is a beautifully conceived dramatic novel. Originally published
in three volumes, it succeeds in endowing each volume with its own
surprises and a cunningly contrived climax: it is also deliberately
didactic. However humorously presented, Mr Woodhouse's vale-
tudinarianism is tiresome and self-centred; Mrs Elton's vulgar snobbery
(and her lack of respect for her betters) is wholly inexcusable; Mr Frank
Churchill's good nature and polished ease of manner conceal a lack of
candour and a willingness to give pain to others. Intelligence is better
than stupidity, as the example of Miss Bates makes clear, but active
goodwill is better still. Jane Austen's ironic stance forces the reader to
think about issues; the restriction of the 'world' of the novel, whether
geographical, numerical or social, does not diminish the principles
involved.

Love, or attachment – the word she preferred – had a precise and
perhaps peculiar connotation for Jane Austen. Essentially, it expressed
the quality of affection that might be found between the members of a
happy family. Young men and women who became honourably
attached to one another were something more than siblings, something
less than lovers.

'Whom are you going to dance with?' asked Mr Knightley [of
Emma].

She hesitated a moment, and then replied, 'With you, if you will ask me'.
'Will you?' said he, offering his hand.
'Indeed I will. You have shown that you can dance, and you know we are not really so much brother and sister as to make it at all improper'.
'Brother and sister! no, indeed'.

But it is on the analogy of brotherly love that her feeling for Mr Knightley has been formed. We do not expect passion in a novel by Jane Austen, but we do find a remarkably discriminating judgment about the quality of affection which her lovers display.

Emma is fortunate: she can afford to attend to the ethics of social behaviour. The women in *Jane Eyre* (1847), *Wuthering Heights* (1847) and *Villette* (1853) were less well placed. Jane Eyre and Lucy Snowe had to work for their living; Catherine Earnshaw believed she had to marry Edgar Linton to ensure her material well-being. The tone of the novels of Charlotte Brontë (1816–55) and Emily Brontë (1818–48) is quite different from that of Jane Austen. They wrote out of a bleaker experience of life. Besides, the moral climate of England had changed: a harshness, associated with Evangelical religion, had altered attitudes and manners. The Brontë children had undergone the severity of a Christian education which was obsessed with the nearness of death and the need for repentance. Together as children they had created a vivid kingdom of their own drawn from the exotic and gradiose images which they had seen or read in the pictures and poetry of the time. Not surprisingly, their early experiences, combining external adversity with a warm, shared, secret life of the imagination, nourished their novels. An earlier generation of novelists had written so-called 'Gothic' novels the fantasies of which had touched on the cruel, irrational and selfish elements in blind human action. The fantasies which they had absorbed from these novels, and those which they had themselves created, were refined by maturity into clear and startling images of psychological reality which conventional morality had suppressed or ignored.

Emily Brontë died when she was thirty; Charlotte when she was thirty-nine. The small body of work which they left must represent only a fraction of their potential output. As it is, *Wuthering Heights* is a most remarkable novel, and Charlotte Brontë's novels are scarcely less impressive. The essence of these novels is their recognition of the intensity of human feeling. Jane Austen was always ready to contrast undisciplined emotion with those feelings which could be acted upon because they had been understood. The independence she sought for her heroines was a spiritual freedom: money and position freed them from external constraints; self-knowledge freed them from the great and little passions which destroy life or demean it. The novels of the Brontës treat the passions of women as if they were an uncharted territory: to express feeling is a right women have been denied. Feeling implies action; and action implies equality. Charlotte and Emily Brontë are feminists.

Both *Jane Eyre* and *Villette* are narrated in the first person; *Wuthering Heights* has a complex narrative structure which employs two narrators, one of whom is distanced from the central events of the novel by temperament and social position, while the other is too closely involved in them to be entirely reliable. So framed, the intense feeling and often unbearable action of the novel are attested to by witnesses whose testimony can be sifted and analysed. The extraordinary central relationship of Catherine Linton (as she becomes) and Heathcliff can be seen against the customary behaviour of the stolid locals or against the superficial politeness of the visitor from the city. The novel falls into two parts: in the first, Catherine and Heathcliff, separated by her wilful desertion of him, burn to rejoin one another with the eagerness of a divided organism for which reunion offers a chance of life; in the second, Catherine's daughter and nephew come together in a gentle relationship which civilises him and releases her from an unhappy past. The novel carries no message: a central storm of savage psychic appetite, and of violence against the self and others, gives way to playfulness and serenity. The movement of the novel is, as it were, symphonic: the mood of the music changes, but each movement has its own artistic logic and its place in the whole. But no one who has read Catherine's passionate declaration of her oneness with Heathcliff will ever forget that this pure tint of blood-red feeling is one of the colours of love. Later psychologists would talk more soberly of the links between love and aggression.

Charlotte Brontë's novels, *Jane Eyre* and *Villette*, offer an interesting comparison. In *Jane Eyre* Jane discovers passion and fears it; in *Villette* Lucy knows its power and despairs of sharing it. Even the prose of the two novels is strikingly contrasted. In *Jane Eyre*, young Jane's early anger and sense of injustice are strongly and directly expressed. As a young woman what Jane dreads most is to have missed the chance of a life of feeling:

> It is in vain to say that human beings ought to be satisfied with tranquillity: they must have action; and they will make it if they cannot find it . . . . Women are supposed to be very calm generally: but women feel just as men feel; they need exercise for their faculties, and a field for their efforts as much as their brothers do; they suffer from too rigid a restraint, too absolute a stagnation, precisely as men would suffer; and it is narrow-minded in their more privileged fellow-creatures to say that they ought to confine themselves to making puddings and knitting stockings, to playing on the piano and embroidering bags.

Jane Eyre seeks employment at Thornfield Hall because in the narrow circumstances in which she lives even a change of servitude will have value. She has the dearly won 'independence' which makes her subject to the goodwill of an employer, and there is much in her situation that reminds us of Richardson's Pamela and Mr B—. She is also aware of her dependence on her employer in other ways. Currents of feeling run in *Jane Eyre* which it is difficult to believe were fully understood by its author. Jane's fascination for the masculine power of Mr Rochester is clear enough. But alongside the acknowledgment of Mr Rochester's sexual attraction, there are repeated suggestions of the sinfulness of sexual irregularity and the punishment that must overtake it. In the charades that the guests play at Thornfield Hall the word 'bride' is followed by the word 'well' to form the name for a place of correction and punishment.

When Jane watches in the bedchamber, after the woman she thinks is a servant has attacked a visitor to the house, she notices that the doors of an old cabinet are divided into panels which represent the heads of the twelve apostles and that 'the devilish face of Judas, that grew out of the panel . . . seemed gathering life and threatening a revelation of the arch-traitor – of Satan himself – in his subordinate's form'. And she goes on:

> Then my own thoughts worried me. What crime was this, that lived incarnate in this sequestered mansion, and could neither be expelled nor subdued by the owner? What mystery, that broke out, now in fire and now in blood, at the deadest hours of night? What creature was it that, masked in an ordinary woman's face and shape, uttered the voice, now of a mocking demon, and anon of a carrion-seeking bird of prey?

We know of course that it is Mr Rochester's mad wife who does these things, but it is surely not 'reading things into the book' to see 'this crime' as the possible release of powerful sexual feeling. When Jane looked at Mr Rochester's expression she sometimes saw 'something which used to make me fear and shrink, as if I had been wandering amongst volcanic-looking hills and had suddenly felt the ground quiver and seen it gape'. The volcanic forces that men concealed, the life of action that women longed for, both demanded expression and were forbidden and punishable. Yielding to passion invokes the wrath of God – after Rochester asks Jane to marry him the great horse-chestnut at the bottom of the orchard is split by lightning: repressing it (as the example of St John Rivers shows) leads to a living death. For all her talk of independence, Jane cannot live alone. The point is well made by her dismay at her cousin, Elizabeth Reed, whose idea of independence is to become a nun.

In *Villette* Charlotte Brontë, through the character of Lucy Snowe, faces the possibility of enduring an independence such as this. Her early experiences of dependence have frozen the currents of her emotions. *Villette* is the story of her return to life through her growing love for a charismatic male teacher who works with her in Brussels (or Villette): her rigidly controlled admission of feeling is contrasted with the warm and happy affection between her old friends Graham Bretton and Paulina de Bassompierre. As Lucy says of them:

> I think it is deemed good that you two should live in peace and be happy – not as angels, but as few are happy amongst mortals. Some lives *are* thus blessed: it is God's will: it is the attesting trace and lingering evidence of Eden. Other lives run from the first another course. Other travellers encounter weather fitful and gusty, wild and variable – breast adverse winds, are belated and overtaken by the early closing winter night. Neither can this happen without the sanction of God; and I know that, amidst His boundless works is somewhere stored the secret of this last fate's justice.

This wan and stifled submissiveness is very far from the rebelliousness of Jane Eyre. The prose that was rapid, direct and exuberant has acquired a strained and brittle artfulness. It no longer has the form of a direct address to the reader: it is a remote deliberate form of self-communing which reads like the introverted journal of a solitary ascetic; it is the rhetoric of masochism. Consider the following:

> It is right to look our life-accounts bravely in the face now and then, and settle them honestly. And he is a poor self-swindler who lies to himself while he reckons the items, and sets down under the head – happiness, that which is misery. Call anguish – anguish, and despair – despair; write both down in strong characters with a resolute pen: you will the better pay your debt to Doom. Falsify, insert 'privilege' where you should have written 'pain', and see if your mighty creditor will allow the fraud to pass, or accept the coin with which you would cheat him. Offer to the strongest – if the darkest angel of God's host – water, when he has asked blood – will he take it? Not a whole pale sea for one red drop.

It ought to be possible to dismiss this kind of writing as false – as contrived and artificially 'poetical'. The formality of the prose, its care for rhythm and for figures of rhetoric (the balanced repetition of 'anguish' and 'despair', the antithesis of 'happiness' and 'misery', the personification of 'Doom') scarcely seem appropriate for the pain and suffering which are its subject-matter. We become impatient with this elaborate attempt to control feeling, only to be struck by the wretchedness it is hopelessly trying to deal with. When we realise that the dark angel is Azrael, who, according to legend, brought God the raw substance for making mankind and was then given the task of separating the soul from the body at death, we can appreciate the significance of what is being said: each moment of life is a time of judgment; no human contrivance can evade the payment of an endless tribute of pain.

Villette is a disturbing work: Lucy's story is a kind of hallucinatory idyll, a piece of wish-fulfilment that Charlotte Brontë does not quite allow to end happily. (The ending of the book leaves the reader in suspense: Paul Emmanuel has shown that he loves Lucy, but he has gone on a voyage. It is not clear that he will come back alive.) *Villette* has a surrealist quality: one of the central episodes takes place when Lucy is in a drug-induced waking trance. Charlotte Brontë's fantasies, her deep longings for a union of mind and spirit, have clashed with her dogged adherence to fact and probability, her sense of guilt and her need for punishment, to produce a strange mannered masterpiece, which has more in common with the work of the American poet, Emily Dickinson (1830–86) than with anything in fiction.

George Eliot's *The Mill on the Floss* (1860) brings us back to a commoner reality. Maggie Tulliver's childhood is wonderfully evoked. Her tantrums and self-will are set against the background of the commercial town of St Ogg's, where her mother's family garner their possessions in a solid bourgeois spirit. George Eliot shows us the plight of a bright lively girl whose ability counts against her because she can do what only boys are supposed to do. But she has in addition inherited her father's impetuous temper, and *The Mill on the Floss* is the story of its taming. As a background to Maggie's story is the account of her father's hasty dealings with the law. The recurrent theme of George Eliot's novels is human egotism: because of its dangerous properties she is unable to countenance unbridled human freedom.

When Maggie grows up she falls in love first with the clever but crippled son of her father's enemy, Lawyer Wakem, and then with the charming but unreliable Stephen Guest. Maggie loves Philip Wakem as a brother (he is nearer to her in temperament than her own brother, Tom) but she is obviously aware of some physical distaste for him. Her efforts at religious self-discipline seem to Philip (and the reader) a destructive self-suppression, but when she allows Stephen to lead her into an elopement acquiesced in by part of her mind, she realises the nature and strength of her feelings for him. She is also aware of the damage they might do to others – especially to Lucy Deane to whom Stephen has been engaged.

George Eliot cannot quite deal with the dilemma she has created for Maggie, but *The Mill on the Floss* is a superb account of the problems of being a woman in mid-Victorian England. A nature eager for life is thwarted by personal scruples, public conventions, religious imperatives and the simple anger of her outraged brother. George Eliot's description of the ease with which Maggie finds herself drifting into doing what she believes is wrong is masterly. Her analysis of why she turns back is equally penetrating: despite her awareness of her own weakness – she longs for the supporting arm that Stephen is very willing to offer – she is constrained by the pressure of long-standing memories and affections which it would grieve her to break. To do so would be a wanton act of violence against her friends and family – and against herself. Maggie has the strength of mind to stand by the choice she finally makes, but she finds it more difficult to face the loneliness and disgrace which her conduct has brought upon her. It appears that the rather melodramatic death George Eliot arranges for her is preferable.

In 1872 George Eliot published her greatest novel *Middlemarch*: there she has little to offer that suggests any improvement in the social position of women. Indeed, she argues, it is the constitution of society which renders their lives ineffective. Dorothea Brooke is a young woman facing her destiny: she has money, good looks and social position. How is she to dispose of her life? In preference to a conventional, but honourable and energetic, landowner, she chooses to marry a desiccated scholar in the belief that she can help him with his work. The marriage is disastrous: she comes to understand what sacrifice she has made of her natural feelings, and Mr Casaubon's work is a laborious sham. After his death, which saves her from a lifetime of self-sacrifice, Dorothea marries a man whose main merit is that she loves him. The climax of the novel occurs before the scene in which she indicates to Will Ladislaw that she is prepared to give up the fortune she has inherited from her late husband in order to marry him. During a night of wakefulness in which she believes she has lost Will for good, Dorothea acknowledges to herself the strength of her feeling for him and, looking out of the window, she sees on the road

> a man with a bundle on his back and a woman carrying her baby; in the field she could see figures moving – perhaps the shepherd with his dog. Far off in the bending sky was the pearly light; and she felt the largeness of the world and the manifold wakings of men to labour and endurance. She was part of that involuntary, palpitating life, and could neither look out on it from her luxurious shelter as a mere spectator, nor hide her eyes in selfish complaining.

Some sacrifice is demanded of Dorothea but it is not the complete sacrifice of self which George Eliot often seems to recommend to her heroines. What she has to sacrifice is her ideal of a life dedicated to some purpose which will ennoble it. To join the working, suffering, active 'field full of folk', which she sees through her window she must be content to be as insignificant as they are. She sees the man, woman and child as symbolic of the destiny she might be tempted to refuse. She might choose to keep her husband's money and resign herself to looking on at life; she might waste her energy in fruitless complaining about her husband's will. She does neither; she accepts Will Ladislaw's offer of marriage and prepares herself to 'learn what everything costs'.

'Far off in the bending sky was the pearly light.' We might use these words as a cue to move to *The Rainbow* (1915) by D. H. Lawrence. Lawrence's novel takes the form of a family saga: three generations of Brangwens, Tom and Lydia, Will and Anna and finally Ursula are portrayed in an unfolding sequence which examines the effect of family life and of the hidden pressures of biological factors on the character of the individual. George Eliot, especially in *Middlemarch*, had been concerned to explore ways of thinking about society which were drawn from the study of biological organisms. The individual was likely to be used for the purposes of society in maintaining its existence. Its almost indiscernible 'thread-like' pressures diverted people from their own aims and moulded them to its use. George Eliot's view of social forces is deeply conservative: they are so pervasive and operate at such depth that they defy rational analysis.

In *The Rainbow* the pressures on the individual are more complex. Lawrence has accepted much of George Eliot's analysis but he has added to it the insights of twentieth-century psychologists such as Sigmund Freud (1856–1939) and William MacDougall (1871–1938). Caught in the strong forces which give the simple continuation of the species highest priority, the individual's chance of a distinctive existence is poor. *The Rainbow* imagines how a traditional family, seeking only to maintain and perpetuate itself, might come to consider life in a new way and demand personal fulfilment in the present, rather than defer it to some undetermined future. Lawrence is very successful in suggesting the uncomprehending sense of dissatisfaction experienced by those who have sacrificed their own lives for the continuance of the race. When Tom Brangwen's stepdaughter Anna wants to marry her cousin Will, Brangwen is angry, not simply because he is jealous of Will, but because he suspects that the unfulfilled potentiality which he has handed on to the next generation is once more going to be entrusted to a future generation rather than realised in living a life which will be significant for its own sake. Here is Lawrence's account of what Tom is thinking:

> What was missing in his life, that, in his ravening soul, he was not satisfied? He had had that friend at school, his mother, his wife, and Anna. What had he done? He had failed with his friend, he had been a poor son; but he had known satisfaction with his wife, let it be enough; he loathed himself for the state he was in over Anna. Yet he was *not* satisfied. It was agony to know it.
> Was his life nothing? Had he nothing to show, no work? He did not count his work, anybody could have done it. What had he known, but

the long marital embrace with his wife! Curious, that this was what his life amounted to! At any rate, it was something, it was eternal. He would say so to anybody, and be proud of it. He lay with his wife in his arms, and she was still his fulfilment, just the same as ever. And that was the be-all and end-all. Yes, and he was proud of it.

But the bitterness, underneath, that there still remained an unsatisfied Tom Brangwen, who suffered agony because a girl cared nothing for him. He loved his sons – he had them also. But it was the further, the creative life with the girl he wanted as well. Oh, and he was ashamed. He trampled on himself to extinguish himself.

What weariness! There was no peace, however old one grew! One was never right, never decent, never master of oneself. It was as if his hope had been in the girl.

Here Lawrence tries to make us share the ebb and flow of Brangwen's feelings, the depth of dissatisfaction which lies beneath a surface of complacency, the hope that some Brangwen life will flower into the creative expression of its own individuality.

In Lawrence's view, the instinctual forces of sex work against the creative life of the individual and bear as hardly on men as on women. The marriage of Anna to Will, so eagerly entered into, becomes a battle for mastery until both are exhausted. It is their child, Ursula, the central character of the final part of the novel, who breaks free from the temptations which stifle the personal life. She escapes from a sterile love affair with Anton Skrebensky and at the end of the novel looks forward to a time when the frost of convention will no longer lie on the freedom of the individual to choose his or her own way of life. Lawrence expresses her strength of purpose in a strange but impressive episode in which Ursula goes out 'to walk abroad, lest the house should suffocate her'.

Making on towards the wood, she saw the pale gleam of Willey Water through the cloud below, she walked the open space where hawthorn trees streamed like hair on the wind and round bushes were presences showing through the atmosphere. It was very splendid, free and chaotic . . . .

Suddenly she knew there was something else. Some horses were looming in the rain, not near yet. But they were going to be near. She continued her path, inevitably. They were horses in the lee of a clump of trees beyond, above her. She pursued her way with bent head. She did not want to lift her face to them. She did not want to know they were there. She went on in the wild track.

She knew the heaviness of her heart. It was the weight of the horses. But she would circumvent them. She would bear the weight steadily, and so escape. She would go straight on, and on, and be gone by.

Suddenly the weight deepened and her heart grew tense to bear it. Her breathing was laboured. But this weight also could she bear. She knew without looking that the horses were moving nearer. What were they? She felt the thud of their heavy hoofs on the ground. What was it that was drawing near her, what weight oppressing her heart? She did not know, she did not look . . . .

But the horses had burst before her. In a sort of lightning of knowledge their movement travelled through her, the quiver and strain and thrust of their powerful flanks, as they burst before her and drew on, beyond.

She knew they had not gone, she knew they awaited her still. But she went on over the log bridge that their hoofs had churned and drummed, she went on, knowing things about them. She was aware of their breasts gripped, clenched narrow in a hold that never relaxed, she was aware of their red nostrils flaming with long endurance, and of their haunches, so rounded, so massive, pressing, pressing, pressing to burst the grip upon their breasts, pressing forever till they went mad, running against the walls of time, and never bursting free.

Only a long quotation will do justice to the powerful impression made by Lawrence's description of instinctive forces which are not controlled by conscious purpose. The horses are constrained by their physical nature to actions which are unfathomable, and inexplicable in terms of purpose and intention. Equally strong feelings threaten Ursula, but she has the ability to find a way past them.

Lawrence's optimism about the possibility of human freedom is unusual. It is not shared by Hardy whose *Jude the Obscure*, considered from the point of view of Sue Bridehead, is relevant here. So, too, is his *Tess of the d'Urbervilles* (1891) which is a profound and beautiful study of the frustration of human intention by fantasy and by the harshness of human conventions. Tess and Clare are in part victims of their misperceptions of each other: their story is a particular example of a general human disposition to believe (erroneously, in Hardy's view) that the world has been created for the benefit of mankind. Tess is a figure of deep pathos, part Eros unfulfilled, part Agape unrecognised.* A more complete consideration of the topic might also include *The Odd Women* (1893) by George Gissing (1857–1903) and *Ann Veronica* (1909) by H. G. Wells (1866–1946). *The Odd Women* is a satirical account of the New Woman of the end of the century, who wanted to be independent of men. Indeed, given the imbalance of the sexes at the time, a proportion of women could not hope to find the security in marriage that had been their traditional aim. As one of the characters in this novel says,

*Eros: in Greek myth, the god of sexual love.
Agape: a Greek word for the spirit of fellowship which united early Christians.

'... Do you know that there are half-a-million more women than men in this happy country of ours?'

'Half-a-million!'

... 'Something like that they say. So many *odd* women – no making a pair with them. The pessimist calls them useless, lost, futile lives. I, naturally – being one of them myself – take another view. I look upon them as a great reserve. When one woman vanishes in matrimony, the reserve offers a substitute for the world's work. True, they are not all trained yet – far from it. I want to help in that – to train the reserve.'

But married women are not idle', protested Monica.

'Not all of them. Some cook and rock cradles.'

In fact Monica marries to escape poverty and dies after giving birth to the child of the husband whom she has deserted because of his protectiveness. He thinks she has been unfaithful to him and doubts whether the child is his. The other character is drawn into an engagement by a man who hopes her advanced views will allow him to dispense with a marriage ceremony. Feminism, in Gissing's view, is a second best, a cause which masks personal inadequacy.

Ann Veronica by H. G. Wells is an engagingly written novel which introduces us to the London of the New Woman, the Fabian Society and the suffragette movement with some of the sharpness of detail of Thackeray's descriptions of London of the 1840s. Ann Veronica chooses independence, though she owes her financial security to an older man who shocks her by demanding the reward which he thinks is due to him. She does not believe in a war between the sexes, however. She has no wish to be protected from the man she really loves: if she found such a man, she says, she would 'take whatever he gave'.

Some more ambiguous aspects of the feminist movement are treated in *The Bostonians* (1886) by Henry James (1843–1916). His *Washington Square* (1880) and *The Portrait of a Lady* (1881) offer darker pictures of disappointed expectations of romance. In *Washington Square* Catherine Sloper's experience of her suitor's prudential calculations persuades her to choose a single life; in *The Portrait of a Lady* Isabel Archer chooses to endure the loveless marriage she has contracted with a fortune-hunter. Many other novels on the theme of women's expectations of life are worth mentioning: *The Old Wives' Tale* (1908) by Arnold Bennett (1867–1931) is a memorable study of the contrasted life-histories of two sisters whose characters are more affected by their childhood environment than by anything that happens to them in later life. In *Mrs Dalloway* (1925) and *To the Lighthouse* (1927) Virginia Woolf (1882–1941) uses modernist techniques to render the inner processes of thought, feeling and memory which constitute the consciousness of women not unlike their author, cultivated, intellectual, sensitive, middle-class, who are conscious of the limitations which their education has imposed upon them and concerned to find ways of reconciling an active participation in life with the meditative contemplation of it. The role of women in society has remained a fruitful theme for novelists such as Rebecca West (1892–1983), Christina Stead (*b*.1902) Rosamond Lehmann (*b*.1903), Doris Lessing (*b*.1919) and many others.

Even such a rapid discussion of two of our chosen themes may have indicated the possibilities which lie in the thematic study of the novel as against the history of its form. It is not easy to convey an adequate impression of the variety of styles which authors have used to represent the sense of reality at different periods of history. The changing assumptions of society are reflected not only in the novelists' subject-matter but in the variations of tone and attitude which are embodied in the language they have used. The written word has very considerable power to offend: actions, attitudes and, above all, language which are accepted in private may cause offence when they are disclosed in public. Until recent times the function of the novel has very largely been the progressive extension of what may be discussed in public – very often in the face of official censorship or legal action undertaken by the state or by private citizens who believe in standards of 'purity' which contemporary novelists may regard as hypocritical: Charles Reade (1814–84) who tackled social problems in the nineteenth century, Hardy, Lawrence, Wells, and Joyce are only some of the writers who have fallen foul of public opinion or of the law. From the time of Thackeray until today the novel has attempted to come as close as possible to expressing 'realities' of every kind from an ever-widening range of points of view.

Love and marriage

The themes which remain must be treated more summarily, since some of the works discussed fall under more than one of our proposed headings. Many novels deal with love and marriage; these are the standard subjects of the nineteenth-century novel, though for most of them marriage is the point towards which the novel is directed, its climax, or dénouement. It might be said that the aesthetically most satisfying form of the novel consists in an initial situation complicated by love problems the resolution of which brings the novel to a satisfactory close. In *Pride and Prejudice* (1813) by Jane Austen, the famous opening sentence ('It is a truth universally acknowledged, that a single man in possession of a good fortune, must be in want of a wife.') almost wearily sets out the terms of the conventional bargain to be struck between the parties involved. Sexual need and sexual attractiveness are brought into balance with the need for financial security and social position. It is taken for granted that the men and women concerned will belong to a well-defined spectrum of society which excludes the highest and lowest classes of society. The setting is the prosperous southern counties of England where the owners of landed estates, not always of gentle birth, hold a strictly regulated social intercourse with clergymen, lawyers, members of parliament, officers of the army or navy, and occasionally with medical men or with those, who, having acquired money by means of trade, are now in a position to devote their time and energy to being gentlemen. As Anthony Trollope (1815–82) puts it in *Dr. Thorne* (1858),

> England a commercial country! Yes; as Venice was. She may excel other nations in commerce, but yet it is not that in which she most prides herself, in which she most excels. Merchants as such are not the first men among us; though it perhaps be open, barely open, to a merchant to become one of them. Buying and selling is good and necessary; it is very necessary, and may, possibly, be very good; but it cannot be the noblest work of man; and let us hope that it may not in our time be esteemed the noblest work of an Englishman.

With the notable exception of Dickens, it is roughly speaking true that the English novel from *Sense and Sensibility* (1811) to *Daniel Deronda* (1876) deals with the love affairs of men and women of this kind of society, and that this concern has a kind of posthumous existence in the English novels of Henry James. Novels such as *Pride and Prejudice* (1814) or *Dr. Thorne* or *Wives and Daughters* (1866) by Mrs Gaskell (1810–65) work within these conventions and are both formally satisfying and interesting as discussions in fictional form of how rational human values can be accommodated to the irrational human desire for sex and money. Two novels may be singled out as outstanding explorations of the institution of marriage – George Eliot's *Middlemarch* (1872) and D. H. Lawrence's *Women in Love* (1920).

In *Middlemarch* four central narratives of love and marriage are woven together into one of the greatest novels of the nineteenth century. The courtship and marriage of Dorothea Brooke to the scholarly Mr Casaubon is followed after his death by Dorothea's realisation that she loves and wants to marry an impecunious young cousin of her late husband: Dorothea's misplaced idealism causes her great grief and by a skilful use of metaphor George Eliot suggests the degree of marital unhappiness which Dorothea suffers. Her wish to be good is portrayed as a subtle form of egotism, which only a willingness to share the common troubles of humanity can remedy. In the third relationship, which is described at length, the sexual blindness of the young doctor Tertius Lydgate is tragically exploited by the social opportunism of Rosamund Vincy. George Eliot's analysis of the combined effect of their mutual incomprehension is penetrating and moving. Lydgate's disinterested pursuit of medical science is thwarted by the unintended consequences of choices which minister only to a small part of his conscious aims. As a repeated motif of the language of the novel makes clear, Lydgate never does what he means to do. The fourth love story follows the conventional form of many nineteenth-century novels: two young people, Mary Garth and Fred Vincy, friends from childhood, are in danger of being divided by money, family ambitions and by the honest feelings that a local clergyman, Mr Farebrother, has for Mary. Fred's own weakness of character almost destroys Mary's love for him, and it is only when he buckles down to a life of honest work with Mary's father, Caleb Garth, that they are finally united on a basis of mutual affection and trust. Fred's and Mary's courtship and marriage provide a conventional background to the more searching stories of Dorothea and Lydgate, with whom the sympathies of the reader are mainly engaged. The Garth family display the qualities of hard work, good will and a sense of community which belongs to George Eliot's earlier fiction and which she seems to have despaired of in the England of the 1870s.

In *Women in Love* there is a more pronounced sense of the disintegration of the social order and of the loss of human values in an increasingly mechanised society. The novel deals with the relationship between Ursula Brangwen, who first appeared in *The Rainbow*, and Rupert Birkin; and between Ursula's sister, Gudrun, and Gerald Crich, the son of a local coal-owner. In the story of Rupert and Ursula, Lawrence explores the possibilities and problems of maintaining a sense of personal identity within marriage and of achieving a balanced relationship in which neither partner is subject to the other. Lawrence tries to define a passionate and exclusive sexual relationship which allows freedom to those aspects of the personality which are unrelated to it. The affair between Gudrun and Gerald illustrates the consequences of a love which is purely possessive and is in fact a marked form of destructive aggression. In addition to these relationships, part of the narrative explores a more advanced stage of the pathology of sadistic love in the feelings Hermione Roddice has for Birkin; another part of it probes the possibility of a close bond between the two men, which is desired by Rupert but not understood by Gerald. After Gerald's death in the Alpine snows, Rupert is left to mourn a blighted friendship, and the novel ends with the counterpoised marriage of Rupert to Ursula, free but interdependent, about to begin.

Middlemarch and *Women in Love* provide an illuminating comparison: each novelist by quite different literary methods undertakes a subtle and searching psychological analysis of what men and women need from one another within carefully considered social contexts. *Middlemarch* looks back with some nostalgia to a perhaps mythical past when the values and institutions of society were sufficiently sound to provide an ordered framework for the satisfaction of human aspirations: *Women in Love* resolutely faces a fragmented and inauspicious social order in which individuals must create for themselves ways of living and codes of personal behaviour to which they can freely commit themselves.

The family

The family is the basic unit of social cohesion in the nineteenth-century novel: in the twentieth it is much more likely to be a chrysalis which must be ruptured before the free individual can emerge. For Jane Austen in *Mansfield Park* (1814) the house from which the novel takes its name represents standards of loyalty, truth, dutifulness and respect for tradition which Fanny Price, the unregarded orphan, absorbs into the structure of her character and thus demonstrates that she is worthy of being the wife of one of the sons of the house. In all of Jane Austen's novels the family is shown as the source of values, though these may not necessarily be sound. The imperfect sympathies of Mr and Mrs Bennet in *Pride and Prejudice* produce in their children a range of character-types only two of which meet with Jane Austen's whole-hearted approval. In *Northanger Abbey* (1818) the reckless behaviour of the Thorpe family offers a strong contrast to the impressionable but essentially sound disposition of Catherine Morland. In *Dombey and Son* (1848) and in *Little Dorrit* (1857) Dickens writes of inadequate fathers and of the plight of their unsustained families. Again and again in his novels we read of children who are orphans or who are neglected by their parents, the children of Mrs Jellyby in *Bleak House* (1852) being only one example. His families range from the pathetically ill-assorted Wilfers in *Our Mutual Friend* (1865) to the horrifying Smallweeds in *Bleak House*, who are united in their general malevolence. Dickens in *Hard Times* (1854) and Meredith in *The Ordeal of Richard Feverel* (1859) display the ineffectiveness of a code of family discipline based on rigidly rational principles: the education of the heart is more necessary than any merely intellectual or moral instruction. *Silas Marner* (1861) by George Eliot is a simple but telling consideration of the essential qualities of fatherhood, a theme developed in her *Felix Holt* (1866), in which the heroine is obliged to choose which family she belongs to. In *The Way of All Flesh* (1903) Samuel Butler (1835–1902) wrote a bitter attack, based on his own experience, of the Victorian father-figure who saw himself as God's agent on earth. The most powerful attack on the late-Victorian family, however, is to be found in the series of novels which were written by Ivy Compton-Burnett (1892–1969) beginning with *Pastors and Masters* (1925) and ending with *A God and His Gifts* (1963). These take as their subject-matter the struggles for dominance within the large family groups of upper-middle class households. She refined on the techniques of dramatic presentation created by Henry James in *What Maisie Knew* (1897) and *The Awkward Age* (1899) to produce novels written almost wholly in dialogue which is elliptical, witty and laden with the conscious and unconscious cruelty and malice of the speakers.

In *What Maisie Knew* Henry James wrote a fine novel about the developing consciousness of a little girl. *A High Wind in Jamaica* (1929) by Richard Hughes (1900–77) amended the Victorian version of childhood innocence and *The Shrimp and the Anemone* (1944) by L. P. Hartley (1895–1972) is an apparently slight but subtly written account of the fantasies of a small boy locked in a destructive relationship with his elder sister.

The social novel

A handful of novels reach beyond the fate of individuals, couples and families to embrace much larger social groups; the best of these attempt to find some means of representing the principal axes along which the social system may be plotted at a given period of history. The most successful novelist of this kind is fascinated by detail and prodigal with the minute description of the surfaces of things. However, if his work is to be more than a catalogue or a series of snapshots he must attempt to find some underlying principles which give shape to it and make his account of society intelligible. In *Vanity Fair* (1848) Thackeray moves at ease in the commercial world of Mr Sedley and Mr Osborne, precisely tracing their contrasted paths of failure and success. He is at home with the land-owning classes and with the military, in academies and ladies' seminaries, in counting-houses and sponging-houses. The spaciousness of the novel is enhanced by its many references to English trade or conquests in the West Indies, in India, in Africa and in Europe. It is located precisely at a time when Regency recklessness and indifference to censure were giving way to a more rigid public morality. Sir Pitt Crawley and the Marquis of Steyne represent a squalid moral indifference which Becky Sharp tries to turn to her own advantage, but on the sidelines the dowager Lady Southdown and Lady Jane Sheepshanks are actively distributing the religious tracts which herald the advent of Victorian orthodoxy.

Becky Sharp is one of the most striking characters of English fiction, worthy of comparison with the heroes of the contemporary French novel who tried to take society by storm. But however much we may admire the energy of 'the Becky puppet', she is too heartless (especially to her son) to command sympathy. Beyond, and dwarfing the doings of Thackeray's people, is the impersonal movement of history which indifferently initiates and terminates action and life itself.

Dickens's great social novels – *Bleak House*, *Little Dorrit*, *Great*

Expectations and *Our Mutual Friend* – are set against a darker background. His attention is focused more narrowly on the fabric of English society, and London is generally its centre and symbol. In *Bleak House* he moves between the landed classes of the country – the Dedlocks and their circle, representative of the landed class, whose claim to govern the affairs of the country is undermined by its manifest incapacity for doing so – and the world of legal London which stretches from the Court of Chancery to the grubby shops of law-stationers and the garrets of underpaid legal copyists. Dickens's aim is to make connections: in *Bleak House* Sir Leicester Dedlock's place in the country is intimately connected with the slums of Tom-All-Alone's; Lady Dedlock is found dead in the borrowed clothes of a brickmaker's wife at the railings of the pauper's grave where her lover is buried. Running through the novel are the New Testament concepts of Justice and Mercy as alternative aspects of the love of God: in *Bleak House* it is the human travesty of the idea of Justice which Dickens attacks most bitterly. In *Little Dorrit* the social and geographical net is flung wider but the groups of people he describes are inexorably drawn together so that rich and poor, the influential and the insignificant, financier, Government official, engineer, plasterer and rent-collector act reciprocally on one another to create a social machine which denies freedom to its citizens. The elaborate social surface of convention and form which is depicted in the novel is essentially hollow: when Little Dorrit and Arthur Clennam marry at the end of the novel they can find no sentiment which binds them to a community wider than themselves; their only resource is a quiet life of private satisfaction. In *Our Mutual Friend* Dickens's rendering of social reality is more boldly symbolic: the Thames with its freight of drowned bodies runs through the novel as a symbol of social corruption and of the uncertain drift of human life; the dust heaps from which Mr Boffin's fortune derives represent the worthlessness of materialism; the marriage of Lizzie Hexham and Eugene Wrayburn marks a rather desperate attempt on Dickens's part to bring the social classes together. *Our Mutual Friend* contains some of Dickens's most brilliant satire on the ineffectuality, snobbishness and vulgar self-display of the people who mattered in the England of his time. Mr Podsnap sums up the deep-rooted insularity of Englishmen of a certain type: and in Bradley Headstone Dickens shows the murderous resentment that a sense of inferiority can breed.

In *Middlemarch* the affairs of families normally separated by social distinctions become intertwined in a way that reveals some of the motivating forces of English society. Although the novel deals with England on the eve of the First Reform Bill, it was written at a time when new constitutional reforms were under way. George Eliot's main themes are the slowness of change and the indifference of social movement to the efforts or interests of individuals. The social theorising of Dorothea's uncle is exposed as clap-trap and the motive forces of society are as different from its outward pretensions as the religious language of Mr Bulstrode is from his real desire for authority and power. Human beings are too blind about themselves to make any convincing claim to insight about the future course of their societies.

Anthony Trollope's main contribution to the study of nineteenth-century English society lies in the two series of novels he wrote – the Barsetshire novels and the Palliser novels – which deal respectively with the land-owning class of England and with the political and parliamentary interests of that class. His subject is the sympathetic study of the English establishment. In *The Way We Live Now* (1875) he moved beyond the interlocking problems of Church and property to write a sharp satire on the new breed of speculative financiers who, like Mr Merdle in *Little Dorrit*, were adding a new force which threatened to disrupt the complex but stable dynamics of English social life.

Many other novels demand more than a mention. *The Revolution in Tanner's Lane* (1887) by Mark Rutherford (1831–1913) forms a link with some of George Eliot's early work in attempting to look at the political movements which grew out of the long-standing tradition of working-class dissent from the established Church of England and the political order it represented. Henry James's *The Princess Casamassima* (1886) and *The Secret Agent* (1907) by Joseph Conrad (1857–1924) introduce us to groups of urban revolutionaries and anarchists. Conrad's *Nostromo* (1904) and *Under Western Eyes* (1911) are further explorations of the relationship between political and personal values. In *Nostromo* he accomplishes the feat of convincingly constructing an inter-related group of territories in South America, the history and geography of which become vividly real to the reader. By the use of complex time-shifts he helps us to imagine the complexity and irrationality of political change, its dependence upon personal whim and on ideologies which often have little to do with the nature of the situation to which they are applied. The attempt of Charles Gould to preserve the material interests of Costaguana – represented by the San Tomé silver mine – is admirable but it supplies none of the spiritual or personal needs of his wife or of Dr Moynygham, who knows that men must have something to live for even after their bodies and spirits have been broken.

James Joyce's *Ulysses* (1922), which is probably the greatest social novel of the twentieth century, is an attempt to encompass the whole of Dublin society on one day (16 June) in 1904. Stephen Dedalus and Leopold Bloom (representative, perhaps, of younger and older versions of Joyce himself) thread their way through Dublin's streets and are found in restaurants, libraries, newspaper offices and pubs and hospitals. The novel is a triumph of style. Using Homer's Odyssey as a framework, Joyce finds a new language for each episode of the novel which corresponds to the character of its situation: the philosophical meditations of Stephen are learned, allusive and elliptical; Bloom's reveries are rambling, heterogeneous and centred on his own memories and impressions; an episode in a maternity hospital gives Joyce an opportunity to recapitulate the history of the development of English prose as if it were the gestation process of a new style which *Ulysses* itself has brought to birth; the immature fantasies of a schoolgirl are written in the style of a woman's magazine. No novel in English has a denser or more dazzling surface appearance, but Joyce seems to have abandoned any attempt to find an internal structure which might reduce the infinite detail of the book to a smaller set of intelligible concepts. The idea of structure has given place to the concept of a continuously expanding new creation which knows no law but the law of style.

Politics

Some novels have dealt more directly with political and social problems. The early novels of Benjamin Disraeli (1804–81) are social in a rather frivolous sense of the term but in *Coningsby* (1844) and *Sybil* (1845) he conveys some sense of parliamentary intrigue combined with a knowledge of the social disorder which might stem from a politically educated working-class. His solution for the problem of 'the two nations' – the Rich and the Poor – envisages a return to a quasi-feudal alliance between landowners and working men against the common enemy of industrialism. Charles Kingsley's (1819–75) *Yeast* (1850) and *Alton Locke* (1850) attempt to deal directly with the intellectual and political issues of the time, the first against a background of agricultural unrest, the second in the context of the radical politics of Chartism and the plight of the poor of the city. Mrs Gaskell's *Mary Barton* (1848) deals with the slums of Manchester and her *North and South* (1855) brings the harsh attitudes of the free-market economy into collision with Christian charity. In *Hard Times* (1855) Dickens considers Utilitarian social and educational theories in the light of a New Testament parable and George Eliot in *Felix Holt* endorses the view of its hero that it is preferable 'to go shares with the unlucky'. *Beauchamp's Career* (1876) by George Meredith deals with the conflict between personal feelings and the concept of duty towards humanity which is a constant theme of the ideological novel. H. G. Wells's *Tono-Bungay* (1909) and E. M. Forster's (1879–1970) *Howards End* (1910) attempt to deal with the problems of an England which can no longer take for granted the religious and moral values which gave it cohesion in the past and which have been eroded by the techniques of business promotion and of 'development'. In *A*

Passage to India (1924) Forster bases his novel on the incompatibility of the cultures of East and West and on the mystery of the tenacity of local traditions in a universe which is fundamentally inhospitable to human attempts to understand it.

Utopia/Dystopia

Speculative attempts to reshape the social world or to extrapolate disquieting aspects of it to the point of future disaster can be traced back to *The Republic* of Plato (?427–347BC) or to *Utopia* (tr. 1551) by Sir Thomas More (1478–1535). Such works are hardly true novels; in them the impulse to organise, classify and preach takes precedence over the urge to record the diversity of the real. *News from Nowhere* (1891) by William Morris (1834–96) envisages a society in which men are able to develop many sides of their ability, unconstrained by an industrial system which insists on the division of labour. Samuel Butler's *Erewhon* (1871) derives from *Gulliver's Travels* (1726) by Jonathan Swift (1667–1745). The inhabitants of 'Nowhere' punish illness and treat criminality as a disease; they also regard machines as dangerous. Modern society has assimilated some of Butler's thinking about criminal responsibility; it is only beginning to be suspicious about the benefits of technology. *Brave New World* (1932) by Aldous Huxley (1894–1963) sees a special threat to the integrity of the individual in the use of biochemistry as a means of social control. The demands of collective stability in the world Huxley foresees have transcended every individual right and responsibility. Consumerism and the imperative to be happy have produced a childish society, where suffering and achievement alike have been eliminated, leaving the deviant hero of the novel, John Savage, to claim 'the right to be unhappy'. In *1984* (1949) George Orwell (pseud. of Eric Blair, 1903–50) sees the danger to human freedom in politicians rather than scientists. In Britain (or Airstrip One) Ingsoc controls its citizens by totalitarian methods which include monitoring by two-way television screens and the suppression of subversive thinking by the 'thought police'. Even the English language has been replaced by Newspeak in which philosophical or political thinking is no longer possible. The rebellion attempted by its central character, Winston Smith, and his girl friend fails completely in face of the collective power of the state.

Inner worlds

All novels, it might be said, are psychological novels. Samuel Richardson is clearly interested in the psychology of his characters and his epistolary technique allows direct access to their thoughts and feelings; Jane Austen writes about the way her characters come to know themselves and others; George Eliot examines in close detail the means of self-deception which her characters use to conceal the true import of their choices and the motives of which they remain unaware. In *The Egoist* (1879) George Meredith offers a comic account of the kind of self-absorption which George Eliot saw as a source of tragedy.

It is not, however, until the novels of Henry James that the psychological process itself becomes a theme for special treatment. As he explained in the Prefaces he wrote to the 'New York edition' of his novels (1907–9) he chose to make the observations and reactions of a central figure the material of the novels themselves. As he put it in the 1907 Preface to *Roderick Hudson*: 'The centre of interest throughout "Roderick" is in Rowland Mallet's consciousness', and of Isabel Archer's adventures in Europe in *The Portrait of a Lady* he says, 'Without her sense of them, her sense *for* them, as one may say, they are next to nothing at all; but isn't the beauty and the difficulty just in showing their mystic conversion by that sense, conversion into the stuff of drama, or, even more delightful word still, of "story".' The 'story' of Isabel Archer, then, lies not in what she does or what happens to her: it lies in telling how she sees the things that happened to her and how her awareness is changed by them. An earlier example of how he tackled this theme (*Washington Square*) will be examined in greater detail in the next chapter of his Handbook. In his essay 'The Art of Fiction' (1884) James compares *Treasure Island* (1882) by Robert Louis Stevenson (1850–94) with a contemporary French novel: 'One of these works treats of murders, mysteries, islands of dreadful renown, hair breadth escapes, miraculous coincidences and buried doubloons. The other treats of a little French girl who lived in a fine house in Paris, and died of a wounded sensibility because no one would marry her . . . . But one of these productions strikes me as exactly as much of a novel as the other, and as having a "story" quite as much. The moral consciousness of a child is as much a part of life as the Islands of the Spanish Main, and the one sort of geography seems to me to have "surprises" . . . as much as the other.' In *What Maisie Knew* (1897) he wrote his own version of the moral development of a child compelled to grow up between divorced parents in an atmosphere of mistrust and deceit.

In his last three great novels, *The Wings of the Dove* (1902), *The Ambassadors* (1903) and *The Golden Bowl* (1904) James deliberately restricts their action to what is seen and thought by a selected number of characters. In *The Ambassadors* the perceptions are those of Lambert Strether, a middle-aged literary man who is sent from America by his friend and patron, Mrs Newsome, to find out what her son is doing in Paris. Strether finds Parisian life far more civilised than the crudely lurid account of it current in Puritan New England. The novel vividly conveys

Strether's sense of the possibilities of life which age, temperament and cultural background have closed to him.

One of the technical innovations in twentieth-century literature was the objective presentation of 'the stream of consciousness'. By that phrase is meant the random association of sensations, memories and inner speech ('interior monologue') which was assumed to constitute the inner experience of most human beings. That human psychology worked by the chained association of inner impressions was a view proposed by John Locke (1632–1704) and David Hume (1711–76), but the means of representing these states of mind were not developed until much later (though Laurence Sterne was an early pioneer). Charles Dickens was certainly aware of this kind of thinking and represented it in the speech of Alfred Jingle (in *The Pickwick Papers*) and Flora Finching (in *Little Dorrit*) but the technique was not developed fully until James Joyce used it in *Ulysses*. Other writers who used this method of presenting states of consciousness were Virginia Woolf in *Mrs Dalloway* (1925) and *To the Lighthouse* (1927) and William Faulkner in *The Sound and the Fury* (1929) and *As I Lay Dying* (1930).

It is instructive to compare Alfred Jingle with Leopold Bloom (in *Ulysses*). Here are Mr Jingle's observations on Rochester castle and cathedral:

> 'Ah! fine place ... glorious pile – frowning walls – tottering arches – dark nooks – crumbling staircases – Old cathedral too – earthy smell – pilgrim's feet worn away the old steps – little Saxon doors – confessionals like money-takers' boxes at theatres – queer customers these monks – Popes, and Lord Treasurers and all sorts of old fellows, with great red faces, and broken noses, turning up every day – buff jerkins too – match-locks – Sarcophagus – fine place – old legends too – strange stories: capital.

There is very little difference between that and the following reflections of Mr Leopold Bloom at the funeral of Paddy Dignam, except that Bloom is thinking rather than speaking and is affected as much by memory and conjecture as by immediate experience:

> Well, it is a long rest. Feel no more. It's the moment you feel. Must be damned unpleasant. Can't believe it at first. Mistake must be; someone else. Try the house opposite. Wait, I wanted to. I haven't yet. Then darkened death chamber. Light they want. Whispering around you. Would you like to see a priest? Then rambling and wandering. Delirium all you hid all your life. The death struggle. His sleep is not natural. Press his lower eyelid. Watching his nose pointed is his jaw sinking are the soles of his feet yellow . . . . Bam! expires. Gone at last.

The adventure story

The adventure story derives from the tradition of the picaresque of which an outline has been given in Chapter 2. Novelists from Captain Marryat to Robert Louis Stevenson, including such writers of much-loved boys' stories as W. H. G. Kingston (1814–80) and R. M. Ballantyne (1825–94), wrote novels whose main interest lay in a succession of exciting incidents: *Treasure Island* by Robert Louis Stevenson is a loving re-creation of novels of this kind written by a master stylist. It is a pure adventure story: Captain Flint's treasure signifies nothing but the heaps of coins and bars of gold which are the worthy object of a treasure-hunt. Good triumphs, though evil is only temporarily subdued. There is regret that lives have been lost, but the morality of the novel is carefully adjusted to the pre-adolescent simplicity of Jim Hawkins, the cabin-boy who tells the story.

Towards the end of the nineteenth century, however, tales of adventure lost their innocence. The exotic settings of the novels of Joseph Conrad (1857–1924) provided suitable locations for the complex analysis of how men behaved in extreme situations. In his short novels such as 'The Nigger of the "Narcissus"' (1897) and 'Heart of Darkness' (1902) human capacities, loyalties and fears are thoroughly tested: and in *The Secret Agent* (1907) the power of human love to withstand an absurd and violent world is tested to destruction. *Kim* (1901) by Rudyard Kipling (1865–1936) has all the appearance of a secret service story (akin, perhaps, to *The Three Hostages* (1924) by John Buchan (1875–1940)). In fact, behind the superb portrayal of the shifting surface of Indian life lies a story of the quest for the secure love of dependable adults which the novel's protagonist finds in a Hindu lama and an old Indian woman who looks after him when he is ill.

European history since 1914 has made it impossible for the simple adventure story to flourish in the twentieth century as it did in the nineteenth, but the tradition has remained alive in the thrillers of Ian Fleming (1908–64), in the novels of Alistair Maclean (*b.*1922), in which a cross-section of types are placed in various extremities, or in the period pastiches of George MacDonald Fraser (*b.*1925) who turned the school bully of a nineteenth-century novel (*Tom Brown's Schooldays*, 1857) by Thomas Hughes (1822–96) into the hero of his *Flashman* series.

Graham Greene (*b.*1904) has followed Conrad in using the adventure story for philosophical purposes. Outstanding among his novels are *Brighton Rock* (1938), *The Power and the Glory* (1940), *The Heart of the Matter* (1948) and *A Burnt-Out Case* (1961). What activates Greene's imagination is the mystery of human love which serves as an analogue for the love of God and which is expressed more effectively in the actions of the simple than in the words of those who are committed to a creed. The novels of William Golding (*b.*1911), *Lord of the Flies* (1954), *The*

Spire (1964), *Rites of Passage* (1981), often draw on the material of exploit or adventure but their themes are metaphysical. Boys' adventures on a deserted island, the building of a cathedral spire, an eighteenth-century voyage to Australia form the mould into which are poured speculations about the incorrigible corruptibility of the human will.

The material of the novel is endless and as varied as human experience and speculation can make it. These thematic nets have caught a number of the significant and memorable novels of the nineteenth and twentieth centuries but beyond them lie the open seas of the novel in English, the European novel and beyond. From the specimens caught and measured here may perhaps be judged the richness of the whole. Theme, however, means little on its own: what interests reader and writer is how the material is treated. In the discussion of the novels we have so far considered, it has always been assumed that what matters above all is the successful realisation in what Jane Austen called 'the best chosen language' of the theme the novelist has selected. What that process amounts to is the topic of Chapter 4.

Technique: reading and writing a novel

Introduction

In Chapter 1 reference was made to the work of Wolfgang Iser on the process of reading a work of literature: reading, according to Iser, is an active process which consists in making an interpretation of the meaning of a text which cannot be considered complete without the reader's contribution. Unlike, say, legal documents, literary texts are 'open'; there are gaps in the meaning which the reader must supply. Literary texts are not constructed to evade interpretation; they invite – indeed, require – it. Many-layered and polysemous ('having more than one meaning'), they can only speak for themselves. There is no extraneous direction about how they are to be understood. If there were such a direction – even from the author himself – it would have no special force to compel assent. As D. H. Lawrence put it, 'Never trust the artist; trust the tale.'

Iser has suggested several perspectives by means of which novels are to be understood: they include the narrator, the plot, the characters and 'the fictitious reader'. None of these elements is to be taken in isolation as the bearer of the meaning of the work: there is a point from which they may be seen to intersect, and it is at this point of intersection (a point of intellectual synthesis) that the meaning is to be found. The elements of the novel which have been mentioned (and some others which will be discussed later) are to be regarded as witnesses to its meaning. Each witness has something distinctive to submit to the reader's under-standing: a careful student of the text will be keen to identify the witnesses, to listen to what they have to say, to think critically about the evidence which is presented and to find the point of balance where coherence and intelligibility are made evident.

The business of this chapter is to survey a number of channels of meaning which have been developed during the course of the history of the novel. These technical developments have accompanied a growing awareness of the complexity of the processes of seeing and telling. During the nineteenth century a principal preoccupation of philosophy and psychology has been our knowledge of the external world and how we could be supposed to know the contents – or even the existence – of other minds. Fiction has not been unaware of these questions; its techniques have been devised to overcome objections to naïve attitudes about story-telling. After a discussion of some of the main issues concerning the nature of fiction, it will be appropriate to consider how to apply theoretical knowledge to specific cases.

The novel and the story

A preliminary matter is to distinguish between the novel and the story. The first of these terms refers to the finished book as we read it from beginning to end. The 'story' is an abstract idea which probably has no existence outside the reader's effort to reconstruct it. The story is simply the action in chronological order, beginning at the beginning and ending at the end. Novels may not follow this order: indeed they may consist of many stories – as many stories as there are characters – which are woven together to create the novel without any particular regard to historical chronology.

In the novel some stories will be regarded as more interesting or more salient than others. In *Emma*, for example, it is Emma's story which is of first importance; Harriet Smith's story is of less consequence, but we can easily imagine Harriet as the centre of a novel by Jane Austen in which Emma was a distant or less favourably treated character. In *Mansfield Park* Fanny Price sufficiently resembles Harriet Smith to provide a hint of how such a novel might develop. Compared with the novel, the story is a reduced and rather ghostly version of the real thing. The novel is the story as it is seen through the eyes of the novelist: it comes imbued with his ways of thinking and of expressing himself. Steeped in the writer's imagination, the story has assumed a form and colour which render it quite different from any summary of it. It has a rhythm, a pattern and a sense of unity.

Normally, its sense of unity depends on the reader's step-by-step assimilation of a number of parts or sections, which taken together make up the whole. Sometimes the number and arrangement of these parts have been determined by factors which were not intrinsic to the writing of the novel: the three-volume novel and the novel published in twenty parts were methods of publication which suited the publishers or the booksellers or the reading habits of the public, but they had a considerable effect on the internal arrangement of the parts of the novel which is still evident when we read in one volume novels which have originally been published in other forms. The student, then, studies the novel in its entirety. He (or she) is aware of the relation of part to part – of chapter to chapter, or book to book. In *Hard Times* (1854) by Charles Dickens, the novel is divided into three books: one is called 'Sowing', one 'Reaping', one 'Garnering'. Each of these titles is a reference to a parable from the New Testament which, if the reader is familiar with it, will shed light on the meaning of the novel. (In his own day Dickens could take such knowledge for granted.) Jane Austen used the three-volume form in which most of her novels were published as if each volume were the act of a play. In Henry James's *The Golden Bowl* Book One, entitled 'The Prince', is distinguished from Book Two, entitled 'The Princess', by a shift in the point of view from which the story is told.

Novelists, for their own reasons, have many ways of arranging and presenting their material. To talk of 'story' is a convenient way of referring to the events of the novel in their chronological order, but we must not confuse this construction of our own with the author's way of ordering them in his novel. An author may choose to present his material chronologically, but equally he may not. The reader must always remember that 'what happens' in the novel can never be separated from 'how it is presented' without some loss of significant value. When we summarise, we foreshorten, and we may seriously distort, what the novelist intended us to understand.

The narrator and the novelist

Novels are commonly narrated but there need not be a story-teller. There may be an 'I'-figure who is given the story-teller's role but it is misleading to confuse this figure with the novelist. The narrator in George Eliot's fiction, upon whose analysis and commentary much of the effect of her novels depends, may almost be thought of as an observer who watches gravely and knowledgeably over the fate of her characters. Such a figure will have a presence in the novel, and will make an impression on the reader which may be very different from the historical figure of the novelist. It may be an idealised version of the novelist, embodying his (or her) most deeply held values; it may be a comical or tragi-comical commentator like the rather rueful narrator in *Pendennis*. It may provoke and challenge the reader after the manner of the narrator in *Vanity Fair*.

There is another reason for distinguishing between the narrator and the novelist: the novelist plans the novel and decides how the story shall be told; the narrator is only a part of the design which the novelist has created. The narrator is not necessarily privileged. Sometimes his commentary must be given special weight, but there may be other means which the novelist uses to suggest how the novel is to be understood: the implications of the action itself, the comments of the characters, symbolism and imagery are obvious examples. All of these strands of meaning may support and reinforce one another, but in some works the 'voices' of the novel may not be in agreement. The narrator may be confused or untrustworthy or prejudiced: consider the narrative voices of *Wuthering Heights*, or *The Turn of the Screw*. A striking modern example of the unreliable narrator may be found in *The Good Soldier* by Ford Madox Ford (1873–1939).

Even if there is no explicit narrator, the impersonal third-person narrative will have its own distinctive voice and manner: literary language is rarely neutral.

Plot and structure

Discussion of plot is often confusing because the term is used in a variety of ways. It is common, but wrong in critical discussion to confuse 'plot' with 'story': when used as a technical term 'plot' has nothing to do with the rapid, shorthand summary we provide when asked to say what 'a story' is 'about'. A simple definition of 'plot' which will serve at this stage of the discussion is that plot is the author's design for a novel, in which the 'story' plays a part, as well as the author's choice of language and imagery. The concept of plot was first developed by the Greek philosopher Aristotle to describe the properties of drama. His formulation introduced concepts such as the protagonist, or hero, whose fate is the focus of the audience's attention. The hero may be in conflict with an antagonist in the form of a human opponent or of some abstract concept such as fate; or the conflict may be in his own mind. As the plot progresses we form expectations about the likely outcome of the action. Our attention may be held in suspense as we wait for the climax or dénouement of the plot when the possible courses of action open to the hero at the beginning of the action have been narrowed down to one.

Aristotle believed that the action of the drama should have unity and that the parts of the whole should be interdependent: they should be linked by an underlying mechanism which is sufficient to explain and justify what has happened to the hero of the play. Although the action should have a beginning, a middle and an end, it was not necessary that the presentation of the action should begin at the beginning. Many Greek dramas open at a point of high significance and the narrative of the events which have led up to that point is given later in summary by one of the other actors. Since death or killing was not represented on stage many of the endings of these dramas were reported by a messenger who has been an eye-witness of the tragic outcome of the action.

Many of the concepts described above are clearly relevant to the novel, but it is necessary to be aware of the considerable differences between the critical language of drama and novel. In drama, for example, action means things done and things said: on the stage we see what the characters are doing and saying and we draw our own conclusions. In the theatre of Ancient Greece the chorus provided a commentary upon the action, but this device did not survive in practice in the Elizabethan theatre, in which the actions and words of the characters are very much more open to interpretation. Shakespeare's *Hamlet* is a supreme example of the need to go beyond the words on the page so that appropriate actions and appropriate tones of voice will supply the linking chain of implication which is required to bring all aspects of the play together in a satisfying unity.

Action in the novel is rather different from stage action. It is, of course, narrated, so that the combination of things said and things done is presented through the eyes of a narrator. The immediate effect of this is to limit the reader's freedom of interpretation. The interpretation of events, mediated through the consciousness of a third party, has already been built into the design of the structure of the novel. It is roughly true to say that the novel of the last two hundred years has been concerned with finding ways to restore to the reader the freedom of interpretation apparently denied him by the nature of the form itself. Various methods have been adopted to reduce the dominance of the role of the presenter or narrator in the novels. Among the main devices are the following:

Summary and scene
There is a clear function for summary in the novel as in the drama. Not all parts of the action need be treated in detail, but when parts of the action are summarised it is the case that the interpretative role of the summariser is paramount. In summary, the narrator not only tells us what happened but why it happened. From such an account there may be no appeal. When the writer chooses to present the action of his characters more fully, when he reports the words they used, and the manner in which they were said, the reader is able to draw his own conclusions about the nature and purposes of the speaker which may or may not be validated by what follows. Human conversation is very likely to be allusive, elliptical, vague and open-ended in a way that a summary cannot be. If a novel has more summary than scene, we may expect our reading of it to be less active and more receptive. One of the developing dogmas of the novel towards the beginning of the twentieth century was that summary should always be replaced by scene: generally speaking, this view was expressed in the dictum, 'The novel should not tell, but show.'

Language
When an audience watches a play, it predicts what is going to happen next. It uses the previous words and actions of the characters as a springboard for forming expectations about their future behaviour and about the underlying point and purpose of the play. When reading a novel, the reader forms similar expectations and predictions by the expectations aroused by the words on the page before him. In the novel,

action, character, plot, conflict and climax are all aspects of language. Certainly, the novelist has plans which will determine the ordering and sequence of episodes and the inter-relationship of events, but all of these must be expressed in the language in which sentences, paragraphs and chapters are written.

One of the ways by which a novelist can extend the freedom of his readers is to use a number of linguistic devices, common enough in poetry, but less common in prose which since the beginning of the eighteenth century has aimed at conveying an impression of realistic authenticity. First among these devices is *irony*: a novelist can use it in two main ways in the narration of his novel. He may allow the narrator to use it towards the action and characters of the novel. When Jane Austen writes in the first sentence of *Pride and Prejudice*, 'It is a truth universally acknowledged that a single man in possession of a good fortune must be in want of a wife', she is using an ironic tone which should alert the reader to the comical inadequacy of values which are merely commercial. It does not follow that an initially ironic tone need be maintained throughout the novel: narrative voices may have many tones, modulating from the caustic to the neutral to the committedly sympathetic.

A second way in which a novelist may use irony is against the narrator himself. The narrator's language may be such that some doubt is cast on his trustworthiness or his good sense. If this happens, the reader is bound to look elsewhere for intelligibility and coherence. Either of these techniques will cause the reader to be on his guard: interpretation will no longer be a matter of course. Readers may feel bound to attempt to disentangle the 'true' story of the characters from the version of it given by the narrator, even if the principal route to the truth is through the narrative of a suspect narrator.

Metaphor is an ancient method of discovering new truth. To see an object or an abstract concept in terms of some other thing is to transform the original perception into something new and, perhaps, extraordinary. Metaphor suggests new ways of seeing familiar relationships. Jane Austen wrote her novels in prose which is relatively free from metaphor. In her novels things (including states of mind and states of the world) are what they are. There are norms which regulate perceptions: to see things in another way is to be guilty of mis-perception. Imagination, which she equates with fantasy, may be dangerous; reason and good sense are the only sure guides to a correct apprehension of the world of human relationships. In George Eliot's novels metaphor is used more freely: in *Middlemarch* she draws constantly on scientific and biological analogies which help the reader to see the place of the irrational and unconsidered, the irreducibly animal aspects of human life. In the novels of Dickens metaphor is a way of thinking: in place of metaphors which incidentally illumine there are repeated metaphors which act as the organising concepts of his novels. Prisons, courts of justice, days of judgment, heaps of dust, rivers, cities cease to be ways of referring to features of the world which happen to lie around us; they become ways by which we can understand and perceive the nature of the world – especially the human world of communities and institutions which men and women have made. Metaphor gives place to recurrent patterns of characteristic imagery which may have a symbolic meaning independent of its conventional meaning. D. H. Lawrence has a characteristic imagery relating to flowers which has a quite specific meaning in his work. It suggests singleness, potentiality for growth and achievement, uniqueness and irreplaceability: in the capacity of the flower to grow and blossom Lawrence sees an apt metaphor for the individual's capacity to achieve a unique destiny.

All of these uses of language may come into play during the course of a novel: they may operate together, reinforcing one another; or they may operate independently, forcing the reader to make his own interpretation of their meaning. In Hardy's *Tess of the d'Urbervilles* the narrative commentary may sometimes appear to be at variance with the reported speech and action of the characters; it is also occasionally difficult to reconcile with the characteristic pattern of imagery based on the sun and the seasons or on references to the New Testament which combine to form the complex fabric of the novel.

In a novel all of these means of expression are woven together to form an action which is divided into parts or chapters which may have their own groupings. Most novels consist of more than one action so that the texture of the novel consists of a complex interweaving of many stories, some treated in depth, some less salient, which are brought together under a general explanatory principle which brings all the parts into a coherent intelligible unity.

A definition of plot which may be comprehensive and simple enough to sum up this discussion may run as follows: plot is the design which is implicit in a novel and which is recoverable by the reader's interpretation of the words on the page and the infinite relationships which may be seen among them. But, some readers may object, if the relationships between words are as variable as the definition suggests, is there only one design which may be discerned in any given novel? The answer to this must be 'no': in exploiting the many-sidedness of language, the writer has finally given up absolute control of his work. But he has not given it wholly into the hands of the reader. The final arbiter of the meaning or meanings of the novel must be what the language will permit: this may give the reader very considerable freedom of interpretation, but it does not offer a licence to the reader's will or whim or to the many personal associations which language may have for him. He cannot claim the right of Humpty Dumpty in *Alice through the Looking Glass* who said 'in a rather scornful tone', 'When I use a word – it means just what I chose it to mean – neither more nor less'.

Plot, it appears, is a complicated topic which can mean almost everything that can be found in the novel. Perhaps there is some point in keeping its two meanings in mind: one, which is related to the concept of plot in drama, is limited to the causally linked sequence of events which comprise the action of the novel; the other, for which the word 'structure' is also used, includes all the components of action and language which together make up the design of the novel as a whole and in the interplay of which its meaning is to be found.

Point of view

'Point of view' is the perspective from which a novel is narrated. The action and events of the novel may be presented by a narrator who stands outside the action, as Fielding does in *Tom Jones*. Such a narrator (commonly called 'omniscient') may comment freely on what he reports, offering evaluations of the characters and events, or he may describe the action without comment ('the objective narrator'). A variation of this method is to limit the perspective to a group (or even to one) of the characters in the novel: in *The Golden Bowl* by Henry James the action of the novel is presented first from the point of view of the prince, and then from the point of view of his wife. In *What Maisie Knew* the action is presented from the point of view of a single character, the young girl whose developing awareness of the adult world is the subject of the novel. A development of the single point of view is the 'stream of consciousness' novel in which reality appears only as it is mirrored in the observations, sensations and memories of a single character. Virginia Woolf in *Mrs Dalloway*, Joyce in much of *Ulysses* and William Faulkner in *The Sound and the Fury*, for example, use this technique.

A novel may be narrated in the first person by the central character or by a minor character who plays only a small part in the action of the novel. Such narrators may be 'omniscient' or they may be limited to reporting the speech and action of other characters without having more than a limited insight into their motives and intentions. Sometimes the narrator makes it clear that he is writing a novel and is conscious of the artifices of fiction (Tristram in *Tristram Shandy* is an excellent example of this). Sometimes the narrator appears to be confused by the story he is telling and the reader is obliged to treat his narrative with caution. Usually the writer finds some means of indicating to the reader where the truth of the narrative lies, but occasionally (as in *The Turn of the Screw* (1898) by Henry James) it may not be possible to decide how the narrative is to be understood.

Character

'Action' and 'character' are interdependent terms: as Henry James puts it, 'What is character but the determination of incident? What is incident but the illustration of character?' 'Character' is a troublesome word in literary discussion because it has two main uses, one of which is strictly literary, the other not so. It may be used to talk about the presentation and function of the persons who are involved in the action of the novel, or it may be used to refer to the psychological and moral qualities which they have been created to represent. In *Pride and Prejudice* Mary Bennet is learned, dull and unattractive: she has a part to play in the novel as a contrast to her more intelligent sisters and occupies a place in the spectrum of marriageability which the Bennet sisters collectively represent. She is both a character in the action of the novel and an element in its formal pattern.

In its sense of 'psychological type' the word has been used to mean many things, since it has depended on the psychological and moral understanding of different societies. Superficial character traits may not differ much from century to century but varying explanations have been given of their source and significance. The mediaeval writer believed that surface characteristics depended upon the state of certain fluids in the body. The dramatist William Congreve distinguished this natural temperament (or humour) from habit and affectation: humour was given us by Nature, habit was given by our experience of life and affectation was an artificial notion of what we might become. So a character might be a complex blend of aspects of all three. To the theory of humours have been added the psychoanalytical and psychological speculations of Sigmund Freud (1856–1939) and Carl Gustav Jung (1875–1961). Religious and moral ideas have set standards and goals for behaviour and have laid down rules about the relationship between the self and others. Some philosophers have questioned the unity of the self, seeing it not as a continuous, stable, natural growth but as a discontinuous stream of impressions, insubstantial, divided and unpredictable. All of these views in their time have influenced the presentation of character in the novel.

Considered in its literary function, a character is a fictional person, usually distinguished by a name, who says and does things and is described in various ways. He or she may be an agent whose words or doings have consequences which affect the action of the novel. He (or she) may simply be an observer of the action, or a means by which the action is brought to pass. He (or she) may form some opposition or contrast to the central character. Each character will be situated in relationship to the central action of the novel and will be treated in relation to his (or her) significance to it.

Characters may be described purely externally or the narrator may be permitted to reveal their thoughts and feelings. In some novels the thoughts and feelings of the characters, objectively reported, may constitute the narrative. For the purposes of the novel the true nature of a character may be masked, or misrepresented by the narrator, if the revelation of the true state of affairs is part of the design of the novel. Sometimes the narrative may fail to be specific about a character so that the reader may be given alternative ways of describing his (or her) behaviour. Characters may be invariable or they may change and develop during the course of the novel.

In *Aspects of the Novel* (1928) E. M. Forster made popular the terms 'round' for characters which are described and developed in depth as opposed to 'flat' characters which have a limited scope of action or mode of speech. But though this categorisation is useful, it usually is insufficient to describe the many different functions that characters may have within the design of a given novel.

The 'implied reader'

Just as the novelist may suggest the character of the narrator of the novel, so he may suggest the character of the reader. Some novelists (Thackeray is one) directly address their readers and even suggest their likely reactions and responses. Others may allude to knowledge which is assumed to be shared with the reader and thus imply certain interests or attitudes which have a bearing on the subject-matter of the novel. The language which a novelist uses generally implies a reader who is able or willing to understand it. Some novels may appeal only to learned or linguistically adept readers who have the time, patience and turn of mind to read what the novelist has written for them.

We may use the phrase 'the implied reader' for all those assumptions (social, psychological, moral or literary) which the author has made about his reader, and which have to be granted before the novel can be read successfully. On the other hand, the distance which the reader finds between himself and the 'implied reader' may suggest grounds for making a judgment about the value of the novel.

Setting

'Setting' refers to the part which may be played by location or milieu or historical time in the design of the novel. This is most commonly a reflective or supporting role; it underlies or enhances the nature of the action or the qualities of the characters which form the substance of the novels. Setting may be a means of placing a character in a society which allows scope for the action his nature is capable of, or it may generate an atmosphere which has a significant function in the plot. The London of the novels of Charles Dickens or the moors of those of Emily Brontë or Thomas Hardy are obvious examples of the part setting can play in fiction.

Studying a novel

It is one thing to talk in general terms about the technique of the novelist; it is altogether more satisfying, however, to look carefully at a particular example. It has been the business of this Handbook to take as wide a view as possible of the novel in English, but it would altogether have failed of its purpose if it had not made clear the need to root generalisation in the discussion of individual texts. A handbook to the novel is very different from a handbook to one's motorcycle: the models are disconcertingly different. Motorcycles must have wheels and engines and handlebars to deserve their name: novels may be recognised as such, even if they display striking formal differences from other members of their class. Perhaps all that can be said of novels in general is that they are made of words. To read an unfamiliar novel successfully it is useful to have read a good many others besides. What follows is merely an attempt to put to use some of the critical terms and concepts which have been introduced above.

The entry in Henry James's *Notebooks* for 21 February 1879 reads:

Mrs Kemble told me last evening the history of her brother H's engagement to Miss T. H.K. was a young ensign in a marching regiment, very handsome ('beautiful' said Mrs K.), but very luxurious and selfish and without a penny to his name. Miss T. was a dull, plain, common-place girl, only daughter of the Master of King's Coll., Cambridge, who had a handsome private fortune (£4000 a year). She was very much in love with H.K., and was of that slow, sober, dutiful nature that an impression once made upon her, was made for ever. Her father disapproved strongly (and justly) of the engagement and informed her that if she married young K. he would not leave her a penny of his money. It was only in her money that K. was interested; he wanted a rich wife who would enable him to live at his ease and pursue his pleasures. Miss T. was in much tribulation and she asked Mrs K. what she would advise her to do – Henry K. having taken the ground that if she would hold on and marry him the old Doctor would after a while relent and they should get the money. (It was on this belief that he was holding on to her.) Mrs K. advised the young girl by *no means* to marry her brother. 'If your father does relent and you are well off, he will make you a kindly enough husband, so long as all goes well. But if he should not, and you were to be poor, your lot would be miserable. *Then* my brother would be a very uncomfortable companion – *then* he would visit upon you his disappointment and discontent'. Miss T. reflected a while; and then, as she was much in love with [him], she determined to disobey her father and take the consequences. Meanwhile, H.K., however, had come to the conclusion that the father's forgiveness was not to be counted upon – that his attitude was very firm and that if they should marry, he would never see the money. *Then* all his effort was to disentangle himself. He went off, shook himself free of the engagement, let the girl go. She was deeply wounded – they separated. Some few years elapsed – her father died and she came into his fortune. She never received the addresses of another man – she always cared in secret for Henry K. – but she was determined to remain unmarried. K. lived about the world in different military stations, and at last, at the end of 10 years (or more), came back to England – still a handsome, selfish, impecunious soldier. One of his other sisters (Mrs S.) then attempted to bring on the engagement again – knowing that Miss T. still cared for him. She tried to make Mrs K. join her in this undertaking, but the latter refused, saying that it was an ignoble speculation and that her brother had forfeited every claim to being well thought of by Miss T. But K. again, on his own responsibility, paid his addresses to Miss T. She refused him – it was too late. And yet, said Mrs K., she cared for him – and she would have married no other man. But H.K.'s selfishness had over-reached itself and this was the retribution of time.

As the editors of *The Notebooks* point out (*The Notebooks of Henry James*, ed. F. O. Mathiessen and Kenneth B. Murdoch, Galaxy Books, Oxford University Press, New York, 1961, p. 13), the characters and situation described here bear considerable resemblance to Morris Townshend and Catherine Sloper, who are the central characters in *Washington Square*. James uses the word 'beautiful' of Morris Townshend, as he appears to the eyes of Catherine in Chapter 4, and in Chapter 23 he puts into the mouth of Catherine's aunt the words (or a version of them) which Mrs Kemble used in advising Miss T. not to marry her brother. There are other verbal resemblances between note and novel. Catherine's father is a doctor – though a doctor of medicine. The note says of Catherine 'an impression once made on her was made for ever': in the novel her aunt says, 'She is like a copper kettle that receives a dent; you may polish up the kettle but you can't efface the mark'. The main outline of Mrs K.'s story is retained in the novel – although Catherine never does inherit all her father's money. But the differences between note and novel are very considerable: there are differences of detail and of emphasis. What is striking about the note is the dominance of the narrator. She knows more about the characters than one might expect her to know: Miss T. still cared for H.K. after ten years' absence; Mr K. was only interested in the money; and was holding on in the belief that he would get it; Miss T. was determined to remain unmarried – and so on. Mrs Kemble's story is a closed narrative; it is a moral tale which we might think essentially Victorian. An untrustworthy young man commits a blameworthy act (the breaking of his engagement) which is not to be forgiven. In the first place the narrator *knows* he is unworthy. When he shows that he is so, the narrator has no doubt that he must not be allowed a second chance. When the man does make a second approach, however, he is not refused upon these moral grounds: he is refused because 'it was too late'. Something had changed in the lady herself – not her love for him; that was unchangeable – but something else which the narrator does not elaborate upon or make clear. She (the narrator) concludes that her brother had got what he deserved: his selfishness incurred a just retribution. (Perhaps we might just wonder a moment longer, however, what is meant by 'the retribution of time'.)

Henry James makes something rather different of this story in *Washington Square*. In addition to the two young people and the girl's father, his characters include the two sisters of Dr Sloper and a sister of Morris Townshend. There are one or two other characters who may safely be ignored. The major alteration is that the emphasis of the novel has shifted from Morris Townshend to Catherine Sloper. Her two aunts have unequally divided roles: one of them, Mrs Almond, is roughly the kindly concerned figure that Mrs Kemble makes in her story – with one major difference: she is not censorious. When she is made to utter Mrs Kemble's advice to Miss T., she is not in fact advising Catherine; she is making a neutral but considered judgment about Morris's suitability as a husband for a penniless girl. Mrs Almond is placed at a distance in the perspective of the novel: she has no direct contact with Catherine and Morris; she discusses the difficulties of the young couple with her brother or with her sister, Mrs Penniman.

Mrs Penniman is quite a different matter. She is a central figure in the novel; she represents everything that might be called 'the romantic'. A widow, she has come to live with her brother and has shared in Catherine's upbringing, since the girl's own mother died just after she was born. Mrs Penniman is the embodiment, as it were, of the romantic novel *Washington Square* is not. She has a girlish passion for make-believe and intrigue; she broods; she plots; she strikes attitudes. Her behaviour, totally inappropriate for a woman of her age, suggests how Catherine might have reacted to some of the temptations and pressures from which she suffers in the novel. She is a kind of middle-aged Marianne Thornton – the sensitive sister in Jane Austen's *Sense and Sensibility*. Dr Sloper is also a character who has no place in Mrs Kemble's story. Certainly, he disapproves of his daughter's suitor; he refuses to leave his money to her if she marries him; indeed he even refuses to leave it to her unless she promises not to marry him (rather as Mr Casaubon does to Dorothea Brooke in *Middlemarch*). But Dr Sloper is a complex and many-sided character whose actions are not simply motivated by worldly prudence; in his character there is also a deep desire to hurt – and to watch the hurt of his daughter. Morris, apart from not being a soldier, is not essentially different from young H.K. but in fact we know less about him. James keeps his character hidden, or rather he gradually reveals it during the course of the novel until Morris reaches a level of baseness and ineptitude far beyond what Mrs Kemble suggests of her brother. Mrs Montgomery, Morris's sister, is an independent witness to his character, though once again James uses her sparingly and not without some ambiguity. Catherine herself is perhaps best studied in action.

These then are the characters of the novel: they are not so summarised by James. The point of the novel is the gradual revelation of what changing circumstances will make of them. James believed in keeping his material taut: his plan (as we may imagine from what the novel achieves) was to engage our interest in a very unpromising heroine by making the plot of his novel as full of dramatic tension as possible. He wants the reader to feel the strain of this triangular relationship between suitor, father and daughter: he wants him to be aware of the parallelogram of forces, the cat's cradle of opposing psychological tendencies, which give the novel its power. As he put it in a letter to a fellow-novelist, 'I think your material suffers a little from the fact that your reader feels you approach your subject too *immediately*, show him its element, the cards in your hand, too bang off from the first page – so that a wait to guess *what and whom the thing is going to be about* doesn't impose itself: the ante-chamber or two and the crooked corridor before he is already in the Presence'. The corridors of *Washington Square* are not crooked: the action moves irresistibly forwards: but the tension of the novel lies in the doubt about its direction.

Washington Square is narrated in thirty-five chapters. It covers a considerable period of time, beginning before Catherine's birth and ending when she is a middle-aged woman. The story is told chronologically but it is not all treated with equal fullness; sometimes it hastens, sometimes it is told in considerable detail. There is preparation; there is 'scene'; there is summary; there is retrospect. James believed in presenting as much of his material as possible in dramatic form. Many of the chapters of *Washington Square* follow one another like the scenes of a classical French play: Catherine and Morris: Catherine and her father: her father and Morris. But not all James's action is 'shown' in this way; some is 'told' in summary form or in a retrospective commentary on what has taken place. It is far from being the case that James believed that his 'telling' was less effective than his 'showing'. Essentially, the novel falls into three main parts – an introduction mainly of Catherine and Dr Sloper and of the new setting which James has chosen for his tale – New York; a long middle section which presents in successive scenes the making and breaking of the engagement of Morris and Catherine, including an excursion in which Dr Sloper takes his daughter on a European tour; a short third section describes the twenty years that follow and in the final chapter we see the last meeting of Morris and Catherine which ends with her sending him away.

In considering the linking of episode to episode we are in the realm of plot. The gathering tension of the novel is generated by the attitudes of the three main characters to one another and by the effect on them of the choices which they make. James begins with an initial postulate of Dr Sloper's which never changes: he believes that his daughter is not intelligent, that she is weak and that because of her wealth (part of which is Catherine's by her mother's will, part of which depends on him), she is vulnerable to fortune-hunters. He sees his daughter from a medical point of view; there is a condition to be diagnosed and a cure to be prescribed. He believes it is his duty to save her from unhappiness.

Morris Townshend is the first man who has ever taken notice of Catherine. His rather tentative first visit to the Slopers' house (with the connivance of Mrs Penniman) produces in Dr Sloper a feeling of dislike for Catherine's suitor: on Morris's second visit, when he sees Catherine alone, we are told:

> The visit was a long one; he sat there, in the front parlour, in the biggest arm-chair for more than an hour. He seemed more at home this time – more familiar; lounging a little in the chair, slapping a cushion that was near him with his stick, and looking round the room a good deal, and at the objects it contained, as well as at Catherine, whom, however, he also contemplated freely. There was a smile of respectful devotion in his handsome eyes which seemed to Catherine almost solemnly beautiful; it made her think of a young knight in a poem.

It is now time to listen more carefully to the narrative voice of the novel. It is a prominent feature of the novel, since the first three chapters, which precede the appearance of Morris, are very largely given over to the narrator's summary of what has happened before the point at which James has chosen to begin what is, properly speaking, the central action of the novel. This voice is never flat or uniform; it is full of shades and tones, on which an understanding of the action of the novel depends. It informs, but it also withholds information; it is ironic, sometimes almost caustic; it offers the reader its account of the early career of Dr Sloper with a certain disdainful reserve which is not altogether easy to follow. It puts the reader slightly on his guard.

It is worth looking in close detail at its tone: consider the movement from 'at home' to 'familiar'; the voice hesitates a moment for just the right expression. Consider the way Morris is described – his lounging, his peremptory familiar violence towards the cushion (is that what his familiarity would amount to?), his wandering proprietorial gaze over the furniture, including Catherine. If we were asked to predict what adverb would be most likely to follow the verb 'contemplate' when it was used of the glance of a lover at his beloved, what likelihood would there be of the choice falling on 'freely'? Again we might hear the faintest pause before the voice of the narrator settled on the word. This, then, is the voice, the tone, the vision of an omniscient third-person narrator, but it can easily be seen that the 'point of view' has no fixed locus. It moves from a plain statement of fact to a description of Morris which does not place him in the best light. Even in that first, apparently neutral sentence, the fact that Morris was sitting in the 'biggest' arm-chair may already have coloured our view of him. It comes to rest finally on Catherine: it is her view of Morris which is given in the third sentence. Notice too how the verbs shift from 'was' and 'sat', verbs of simple statement, to 'seemed', which implies an impression, a 'point of view': it is no longer a factual statement guaranteed by the narrator. But it is not until the third sentence that the impression is attributed to Catherine. Having made an evaluation of the impression created by Morris's 'lounging', and 'slapping' and 'looking round', the reader must now consider what is to be made of Catherine's impression of Morris as 'a young knight in a poem'. Dr Sloper in the next chapter (Chapter 7) has no doubt of his own impression of Morris:

'He is not what I call a gentleman; he has not the soul of one. He is extremely insinuating. He is altogether too familiar – I hate familiarity. He is a plausible coxcomb'.

The plot of *Washington Square* is concerned initially with the relationship between Morris and Dr Sloper. Morris knows he is disliked: he tries to arrange a meeting with Catherine outside her home. She refuses. She does not want a romantic assignation; she is quite prepared to meet him in the parlour. When he says, 'We must take a line', she says, 'We must do our duty'. It is at the end of this scene that a crucial episode takes place.

'You must tell me', Morris says, 'that if your father is dead against me, if he absolutely forbids our marriage, you will still be faithful'.
    Catherine opened her eyes, gazing at him, and she could give no better promise than what he read there.
    'You will cleave to me?' said Morris. 'You know you are your own mistress – you are of age'.

'Ah, Morris!' she murmured, for all answer; or rather not for all, for she put her hand into his own. He kept it a while, and presently he kissed her again.

There can be no doubt about Catherine's sincerity. She wants enduring affection and she shows this by the way she looks at Morris and by the fact that she gives him her hand. (Consider carefully the tone of the narrative when it describes Catherine's actions.) What evaluation do we make of Morris's behaviour? When Catherine gave him her hand 'he kept it a while' – 'presently' he kissed her. Not, we may think, the actions of a passionate or a sincerely devoted lover.

Perhaps it is now clear that the plot of *Washington Square* is beginning to tighten and grip – characters, action and the varied tones of the voice of the narrator mesh together to command our attention to the smallest detail of the text. Part of the tension of the plot is generated by the shifting point of view of the narrative, controlled though it is by an objective narrator who makes his own decision about how much of the action he will allow us to see. (The voice is the narrator's, but the controlling hand belongs to James.) The characters of *Washington Square* certainly do not live in a common world: each looks at the situation from a highly personal point of view. James allows us to see Catherine's vulnerability and idealism; he does not immediately show us exactly what Morris is capable of; only gradually does Dr Sloper's amused contempt for his daughter turn to hatred.

Dr Sloper is engaged in a deep game with Catherine: first he believes he can command her to do what he wants; then he believes he can frighten her; then he attempts to withdraw, making believe that he is indifferent. When it is clear that she is adamant and has thought through her position to the point where she believes that she should no longer remain at home, if she intends to disobey him, he decides to take her to Europe. But separation makes no difference to Catherine: she brings back to Morris 'her indiverted heart'. Dr Sloper is equally immovable, but what he shows to Catherine is an absolute absence of love. On the eve of their voyage home he says to her:

'So, as soon as you arrive, you are going off with him?'
. . . 'I cannot tell you till we arrive', she said.
'That's reasonable enough', her father answered. 'That's all I ask of you – that you *do* tell me, that you give me definite notice. When a poor man is to lose his only child, he likes to have an inkling of it before hand.'
'Oh, father! You will not lose me', Catherine said, spilling her candle wax.

As he begins to realise how determined she is to remain faithful to Morris, her father's language to her becomes more violent. He complains to Mrs Almond that Catherine is 'glued' to Morris and that if she does not let go, she will be shaken off – 'sent tumbling into the dust'. He intends to disinherit her if she marries Morris and will break off relations with her. When Morris realises that Dr Sloper does not mean to 'come round', he decides he must give Catherine up.

At this point in the novel Morris, Mrs Penniman and Dr Sloper find common ground in their willingness to sacrifice Catherine: her father is willing to sacrifice her to his belief that he knows what is best for her; Mrs Penniman is willing to sacrifice her because she cannot resist living vicariously in the romantic glamour of Morris's destiny; Morris is willing to sacrifice her because she will not bring him enough money. The effect on Catherine is grievous and James offers a grave and measured account of her grief, when she realises that Morris – on the pretext of a business trip – has left her (although he promises to come back):

> It was almost the last passion of her life; at least she never indulged in another that the world knew anything about. But this one was long and terrible; she flung herself on the sofa and gave herself up to her grief. She hardly knew what had happened; ostensibly she had only had a difference with her lover as other girls had had before, and the thing was not only a rupture, but she was under no obligation to regard it even as a menace. Nevertheless, she felt a wound, even if he had not dealt it; it seemed to her that a mask had suddenly fallen from his face. He had wished to get away from her; he had been angry and cruel, and said strange things, with strange looks. She was smothered and stunned; she buried her head in the cushions sobbing and talking to herself. But at last she raised herself, with the fear that either her father or Mrs Penniman would come in; and then she sat there, staring before her, while the room grew darker. She said to herself that perhaps he would come back to tell her he had not meant what he said; and she listened for his ring at the door, trying to believe that this was probable. A long time passed, but Morris remained absent; the shadows gathered; the evening settled down on the meagre elegance of the light clear-coloured room; the fire went out. When it had grown dark, Catherine went to the window and looked out; she stood there for half an hour, on the mere chance that he would come up the steps. At last she turned away, for she saw her father come in. He had seen her at the window looking out, and he stopped a moment at the bottom of the white steps, and gravely, with an air of exaggerated courtesy, lifted his hat to her. The gesture was so incongruous to the condition she was in, this stately tribute of respect to a poor girl despised and forsaken was so out of place, that the thing gave her a kind of horror, and she hurried away to her room. It seemed to her that she had given Morris up.

This grave, studied narrative of the climax of the novel repays careful study. Its quiet analysis of these unspoken passages of feeling is deeply moving. They evoke the sense of despair, the painful fantasies that persist after the severing of a relationship (as after the severing of a limb). The darkening scene follows the ebbing of hope. Her father's strange gesture reveals his withdrawal of feeling (the gesture mocks her), as if he knew she had been defeated; it is a tribute by a spectator to the sacrificed animal; it echoes a persistent pattern of imagery which runs through the novel which has to do with the theatre, with play-acting and the detached observation of the performance of a play. But more is suggested than the agitation of Catherine's spirit; she has also made a decision. The last sentence is ambivalent: she despairs of Morris's return, perhaps; she has also decided to break with him. Morris's giving up of Catherine is very different from Catherine's giving up of Morris: the motives are different, so is the feeling. What the phrase means depends entirely on its user: it is a question of point of view.

Catherine's story does not end here, but her integrity is henceforward unassailable. She has found a self and a way of living which she means to stick with. James has converted a story about bad faith and its punishment into a novel which movingly describes the ripening of an independent spirit, the painful attainment of personal detachment; *Washington Square* is a partial defeat, a partial victory. Catherine will never recover from her experiences but they have given her the strength to go through life on her own. As she says to Morris at their last interview, 'Impressions last, when they have been strong.'

The impression made on Catherine by Morris Townshend is twofold: on the one hand he represents an image of what love might be, on the other he represents the reality of betrayal and disappointment. When he returns to Catherine at the end of the novel she finds that these first impressions cannot be effaced.

In moving from notebook to novel, James invented a complex action by means of which the character of Catherine Sloper is revealed in its strength and maturity. Although *Washington Square* is not narrated through her eyes, the sympathies of the narrator are closest to her and through a mixture of narrative and objectively presented 'scenic' action we can follow the development of her consciousness, of her sense of self and of her independent acquisition of a set of moral values which will see her through life. James leaves the reader to form an understanding of what these values are; much is to be inferred from the action itself, from the interplay of the interests and motivations of the characters, as they pursue their own purposes and form their own judgments of what is said and done by the other members of the cast of James's drama. Behind them stands the narrator whose tone changes with the changing action. When the novel opens his tone is ironic, complex, ambiguous, uncommitted. As the action developts, involving Catherine more and more deeply in a conflict of loyalties and love between her father and her lover, the narrator's tone becomes more clearly sympathetic to Catherine, but James is careful never to allow the narrative voice to preach or to deprive the reader of the final responsibility of weighing up the motives, actions and qualities of mind and spirit which the characters display. As the novel begins in ambiguity, so it ends. Catherine, having dismissed Morris for the last time, takes up her piece of fancy-work 'for life, as it were'. The reader is left to make what he can of the final ambivalent phrase. Has Catherine condemned herself to loneliness in a spirit of life-denying moral rectitude? Or has she, by dismissing him, laid the coping stone on the fine fabric she has constructed of a life of her own? Crucial to the success of James's novel is his fastidious use of language, which must always be read with the greatest care. When, after her trip to Europe, Catherine brings back to Morris her 'indiverted heart' the reader should be aware that 'indiverted' means both 'what cannot be turned from its course' and 'what cannot be drawn away from serious occupations by amusement or entertainment'. Both senses may appear to mean the same thing, but the first of them refers to Morris, the second refers to Dr Sloper. The European trip does not change Catherine's mind: it unalterably defines her attitude to her lover and to her father. It is in the tension set up between them that Catherine matures from a dependent, awkward, plain but rich girl to a clear-sighted woman whose destiny consists in choosing a life for herself.

By comparing James's notebook entry with his novel, we may become more aware of the distance which lies between the 'story' and the 'novel', between the hints and suggestions from which the novelist begins and the refined, elaborate and many-faceted finished work which he offers to the reader. Such an awareness may save us from the danger of confusing the novel with any summary of it, or of accepting an interpretation of it which fails to do justice to any of the many strands of meaning which make up the complex whole.

A map of the English novel

The following is an outline map of the novel from the sixteenth century to the modern period. Titles of novels are in italics, followed by dates of publication, where known. Significant events, and novels in languages other than English, followed in brackets by their country of origin, appear in the right-hand column.

Significant works of prose fiction written before 1700		Significant events
William Adington (tr.)	*The Golden Ass of Apuleius*, 1566	Spanish Armada, 1588
John Lyly (?1554–1606)	*Euphues and his England*, 1580	Accession of James I, 1603
David Rowland (tr.)	*Lazarillo de Tormes*, 1586	Mateo Alemán (1547–?1614), *Guzmán de Alfarache*,
Angell Day (tr.)	*Daphnis and Chloe*, 1587	1599–1604 (*Sp.*)
Thomas Nashe (1567–1601)	*The Unfortunate Traveller*, 1594	Miguel de Cervantes (1547–1616)
		Don Quixote, Part 1, 1605 (*Sp.*)
Thomas Shelton (tr.)	*Don Quixote*, Part 1, 1612	Part 2, 1615 (*Sp.*)
	Part 2, 1620	Execution of Charles I, 1649
		Restoration of Charles II, 1660
		Madame de Scudéry (1608–1701), *Clelie*, 1660 (*Fr.*)
John Bunyan (1628–88)	*Pilgrim's Progress*, Part 1, 1678	Madame de Lafayette (1634–93), *La Princesse de*
	Part 2, 1684	*Clèves*, 1678 (*Fr.*)
Aphra Behn (1640–89)	*Oroonoko*, 1688	The Glorious Revolution, 1689 (Accession of
		William and Mary)
Sir Roger l'Estrange (tr.) (1616–1704)	*Fables of Aesop*, 1692–9	
Sir Thomas Urquhart (tr.) (1611–60)	*Gargantua and Pantagruel*,	
	Books 1 and 2, 1653	
	Book 3, 1693	

Eighteenth century

Authors	Works	Significant events
Sir Richard Steele (1672–1729)	*The Tatler*, 1709–11 (essays)	Union of English and Scottish Parliaments, 1707
Joseph Addison (1672–1719)	*The Spectator*, 1711–14 (essays)	Accession of George I, 1714
		First Jacobite Rebellion, 1715
Daniel Defoe (?1661–1731)	*Robinson Crusoe*, 1719	Alain-René Le Sage (1668–1747), *Gil Blas*, Part 1, 1715 (*Fr.*)
	Moll Flanders, 1721–2	
Jonathan Swift (1667–1745)	*Gulliver's Travels*, 1726	Accession of George II, 1727
		L'Abbé Prévost (1697–1763), *Manon Lescaut*, 1731 (*Fr.*)
Samuel Richardson 1689–1761)	*Pamela*, 1740	P. Marivaux (1688–1763), *La Vie de Marianne*, 1741 (*Fr.*)
Henry Fielding (1707–54)	*Joseph Andrews*, 1742	Second Jacobite Rebellion, 1745
Samuel Richardson	*Clarissa*, 1748	
Tobias Smollett (1721–71)	*Roderick Random*, 1748	
Henry Fielding	*Tom Jones*, 1749	
Tobias Smollett (tr.)	*Gil Blas*, 1749	
Samuel Johnson (1709–84)	*The Rambler*, 1750–2 (essays)	
Tobias Smollett	*Peregrine Pickle*, 1751	
Samuel Richardson	*Sir Charles Grandison*, 1753	
Tobias Smollett (tr.)	*Don Quixote*, 1755	
Samuel Johnson	*Rasselas*, 1759	Voltaire (1694–1778), *Candide*, 1759 (*Fr.*)
Laurence Sterne (1713–68)	*Tristram Shandy*, 1760–7	Accession of George III, 1760
		J. J. Rousseau (1712–78), *La Nouvelle Héloïse*, 1761 (*Fr.*)
Horace Walpole (1717–97)	*Castle of Otranto*, 1765	James Watt invents the steam engine, 1765
Oliver Goldsmith (?1730–74)	*The Vicar of Wakefield*, 1766	
Richard Graves (1715–1804)	*The Spiritual Quixote*, 1772	J. W. von Goethe, (1749–1832), *The Sorrows of Young Werther*, 1774 (*Ger.*)
		War of American Independence, 1775–83
Fanny Burney (1752–1840)	*Evelina*, 1778	Choderlos de Laclos (1741–1803), *Les Liaisons Dangereuses*, 1782 (*Fr.*)
William Beckford (1760–1844)	*Vathek*, 1786	French Revolution, 1789

Eighteenth century (*cont.*)

Author	Work	Significant events
William Godwin (1756–1836)	*Caleb Williams*, 1794	Marquis de Sade (1740–1814), *Justine*, 1791 (*Fr.*)
Ann Radcliffe (1764–1823)	*The Mysteries of Udolpho*, 1794	War with France, 1793–1802
Matthew Lewis (1775–1818)	*The Monk*, 1796	
Maria Edgeworth (1767–1849)	*Castle Rackrent*, 1800	

1800–1876

Author	Work	Significant events
Jane Austen (1775–1817)	*Sense and Sensibility*, 1811	Napoleonic Wars, 1802–15
Jonathan Scott (tr.) (1754–1829)	*The Arabian Nights*, 1811	
Jane Austen	*Pride and Prejudice*, 1813	
	Mansfield Park, 1814	
Sir Walter Scott (1771–1832)	*Waverley*, 1814	Battle of Waterloo, 1815
Jane Austen	*Emma*, 1816	Benjamin Constant (1767–1830), *Adolphe*, 1816 (*Fr.*)
Thomas Love Peacock (1785–1866)	*Headlong Hall*, 1816	
Sir Walter Scott	*Old Mortality*, 1816	
Jane Austen	*Northanger Abbey*, 1818	
	Persuasion, 1818	
Sir Walter Scott	*The Heart of Midlothian*, 1818	
Susan Ferrier (1782–1854)	*Marriage*, 1818	
Mary Shelley (1797–1851)	*Frankenstein*, 1818	
John Galt (1779–1839)	*The Annals of the Parish*, 1821	Accession of George IV, 1820
James Hogg (1770–1835)	*Memoirs and Confessions of a Justified Sinner*, 1824	
Sir Walter Scott	*Redgauntlet*, 1824	James Fenimore Cooper (1789–1851), *The Last of the Mohicans*, 1826 (*Am.*)
		Stendhal (1783–1842), *Le Rouge et le Noir*, 1830 (*Fr.*)
		Accession of William IV, 1830
		First Reform Bill, 1832
Charles Dickens (1812–70)	*Pickwick Papers*, 1836	H. de Balzac (1799–1850), *Père Goriot*, 1834 (*Fr.*)

Captain Marryat (1792–1848)	Mr Midshipman Easy, 1836	
Charles Dickens	Oliver Twist, 1837	Accession of Queen Victoria, 1837
		H. de Balzac, Illusions Perdues, 1843 (Fr.)
Charles Dickens	Martin Chuzzlewit, 1844	
Benjamin Disraeli (1804–81)	Coningsby, 1844	
	Sybil, 1845	
Charlotte Brontë (1816–55)	Jane Eyre, 1847	H. de Balzac, Cousin Pons, 1847 (Fr.)
Emily Brontë (1818–48)	Wuthering Heights, 1847	
Mrs E. Gaskell (1810–65)	Mary Barton, 1848	'Year of Revolutions', 1848
W. M. Thackeray (1811–63)	Pendennis, 1849	
Charles Dickens	David Copperfield, 1850	
Charles Kingsley (1819–75)	Yeast, 1848	Nathaniel Hawthorne (1804–64), The Scarlet Letter, 1850 (Am.)
	Alton Locke, 1850	Hermann Melville (1819–91), Moby Dick, 1851 (Am.)
		Harriet Beecher Stowe (1811–96), Uncle Tom's Cabin, 1852 (Am.)
Charles Dickens	Bleak House, 1853	
Charlotte Brontë	Villette, 1853	
Mrs E. Gaskell	Ruth, 1853	
	Cranford, 1853	
Charlotte M. Yonge (1823–1901)	The Heir of Redclyffe, 1853	
Charles Dickens	Hard Times, 1854	Crimean War, 1854–6
Mrs E. Gaskell	North and South, 1855	
Anthony Trollope (1815–82)	The Warden, 1855	
Charles Dickens	Little Dorrit, 1857	G. Flaubert (1821–80), Madame Bovary, 1857 (Fr.)
Anthony Trollope	Barchester Towers, 1857	
	Dr Thorne, 1858	
George Eliot (1819–80)	Adam Bede, 1859	
George Meredith (1828–1909)	The Ordeal of Richard Feverel, 1859	
George Eliot	The Mill on the Floss, 1860	
Charles Dickens	Great Expectations, 1861	
George Eliot	Silas Marner, 1861	V. Hugo (1802–85), Les Misérables, 1862 (Fr.)
Charles Reade (1814–84)	Hard Cash, 1863	I. Turgenev (1818–83), Fathers and Sons, 1862 (Rus.)
Charles Dickens	Our Mutual Friend, 1865	Leo Tolstoy (1828–1910), War and Peace, 1863–9 (Rus.)
Lewis Carroll (1832–98)	Alice's Adventures in Wonderland, 1865	

	Significant events
Mrs E. Gaskell — *Wives and Daughters*, 1866	F. Dostoevsky (1821–81), *Crime and Punishment*, 1866 (*Rus.*)
George Eliot — *Felix Holt*, 1866	Emile Zola (1840–1902), *Thérèse Raquin*, 1867 (*Fr.*)
	Second Reform Bill, 1867
Anthony Trollope — *Phineas Finn*, 1869	Louisa M. Alcott (1832–88), *Little Women*, 1868 (*Am.*)
	F. Dostoevsky, *The Idiot*, 1869 (*Rus.*)
George Eliot — *Middlemarch*, 1871	Franco-Prussian War, 1870–1
Lewis Carroll — *Through the Looking Glass*, 1871	Education Act, 1870
Samuel Butler (1835–1902) — *Erewhon*, 1872	
Thomas Hardy (1840–1928) — *Under the Greenwood Tree*, 1872	
Far From the Madding Crowd, 1874	Leo Tolstoy, *Anna Karenina*, 1873–7 (*Rus.*)
Anthony Trollope — *The Way We Live Now* (1875)	
George Eliot — *Daniel Deronda*, 1876	

1876–1980

	Significant events
Henry James (1843–1916) — *Roderick Hudson*, 1876	Mark Twain (1835–1910), *Tom Sawyer*, 1876 (*Am.*)
Thomas Hardy — *The Return of the Native*, 1878	
George Meredith — *The Egoist*, 1879	
Henry James — *The Europeans*, 1879	
Washington Square, 1880	
The Portrait of a Lady, 1881	
Robert Louis Stevenson (1850–94) — *Treasure Island*, 1882	
Sir Richard Burton (tr.) (1821–90) — *The Arabian Nights*, 1885	W. D. Howells (1837–1920), *The Rise of Silas Lapham*, 1884 (*Am.*)
Walter Pater (1839–94) — *Marius the Epicurean*, 1885	Emile Zola, *Germinal*, 1885 (*Fr.*)
Frances H. Burnett (1849–1924) — *Little Lord Fauntleroy*, 1886	
Thomas Hardy — *The Mayor of Casterbridge*, 1886	
Henry James — *The Bostonians*, 1886	
The Princess Casamassima, 1886	

Robert Louis Stevenson	*Kidnapped*, 1886	Emile Zola, *La Terre*, 1887 (*Fr.*)
	Dr Jekyll and Mr Hyde, 1886	
William Morris (1834–96)	*News from Nowhere*, 1891	International Copyright Act, 1891
Thomas Hardy	*Tess of the d'Urbervilles*, 1891	
George Gissing (1857–1903)	*The Odd Women*, 1893	
George Moore (1852–1933)	*Esther Waters*, 1894	
Thomas Hardy	*Jude the Obscure*, 1895	Stephen Crane (1871–1900), *The Red Badge of Courage*, 1895 (*Am.*)
H. G. Wells (1866–1946)	*The Time Machine*, 1895	
Joseph Conrad (1857–1924)	*The Nigger of the 'Narcissus'*, 1897	
Henry James	*What Maisie Knew*, 1897	
	The Awkward Age, 1899	
Joseph Conrad	*Lord Jim*, 1900	Theodore Dreiser (1871–1945), *Sister Carrie*, 1900 (*Am.*)
		Frank Norris (1870–1902), *The Octopus*, 1901 (*Am.*)
		Death of Queen Victoria, 1901
Rudyard Kipling (1865–1936)	*Kim*, 1901	Thomas Mann (1875–1955), *Buddenbrooks*, 1901 (*Ger.*)
Joseph Conrad	*Youth*, 1902	
Henry James	*The Wings of the Dove*, 1902	Jack London (1876–1916), *Call of the Wild*, 1903 (*Am.*)
Samuel Butler	*The Way of All Flesh*, 1903	
Henry James	*The Ambassadors*, 1903	
Joseph Conrad	*Nostromo*, 1904	
Henry James	*The Golden Bowl*, 1904	
H. G. Wells	*Kipps*, 1905	
Arnold Bennett (1867–1931)	*The Old Wives' Tale*, 1908	
E. M. Forster (1879–1970)	*A Room with a View*, 1908	
Kenneth Grahame (1859–1932)	*The Wind in the Willows*, 1908	
H. G. Wells	*Ann Veronica*, 1909	
	Tono-Bungay, 1909	
E. M. Forster	*Howards End*, 1910	
D. H. Lawrence (1885–1930)	*Sons and Lovers*, 1913	
James Joyce (1882–1941)	*Dubliners*, 1914	First World War, 1914–18
Ford Madox Ford (1873–1939)	*The Good Soldier*, 1915	

1876–1980 (cont.)

	Significant events
D. H. Lawrence — The Rainbow, 1915	Russian Revolution, 1917
James Joyce — A Portrait of the Artist as a Young Man, 1916	
D. H. Lawrence — Women in Love, 1920	Thomas Mann, *The Magic Mountain*, 1924 (Ger.)
James Joyce — Ulysses, 1922	Franz Kafka (1883–1924), *The Trial*, 1925 (Ger.)
E. M. Forster — A Passage to India, 1924	Theodore Dreiser, *An American Tragedy*, 1925 (Am.)
Virginia Woolf (1882–1941) — Mrs Dalloway, 1925	F. Scott Fitzgerald (1896–1940), *The Great Gatsby*, 1925 (Am.)
	Franz Kafka, *The Castle*, 1926 (Ger.)
	André Gide (1869–1951), *Les Faux-monnayeurs*, 1926 (Fr.)
D. H. Lawrence — Lady Chatterley's Lover, 1928	Marcel Proust (1871–1922), *A la recherche du temps perdu*, 1913–28 (Fr.)
Evelyn Waugh (1903–66) — Decline and Fall, 1928	Ernest Hemingway (1898–1961), *A Farewell to Arms*, 1929 (Am.)
Richard Hughes (1900–77) — A High Wind in Jamaica, 1929	
Evelyn Waugh — Vile Bodies, 1930	William Faulkner (1897–1962), *The Sound and the Fury*, 1929 (Am.)
Virginia Woolf — The Waves, 1931	Jean-Paul Sartre (1905–81), *La nausée*, 1938 (Fr.)
Aldous Huxley (1894–1963) — Brave New World, 1932	Second World War, 1939–45
Graham Greene (b.1904) — Brighton Rock, 1938	John Steinbeck (1902–68), *Grapes of Wrath*, 1939 (Am.)
James Joyce — Finnegans Wake, 1939	Ernest Hemingway, *For Whom the Bell Tolls*, 1940 (Am.)
	Richard Wright (1908–60), *Native Son*, 1940 (Am.)
Evelyn Waugh — Brideshead Revisited, 1945	Thomas Mann, *Doctor Faustus*, 1947 (Ger.)
George Orwell (1903–50) — Animal Farm, 1945	Albert Camus (1913–60), *La peste*, 1947 (Fr.)

Graham Greene	The Heart of the Matter, 1948
George Orwell	1984, 1949
William Golding (b.1911)	Lord of the Flies, 1954
Angus Wilson (b.1913)	Anglo-Saxon Attitudes, 1956
Iris Murdoch (b.1919)	The Bell, 1958
Doris Lessing (b.1919)	The Golden Notebook, 1962
Angus Wilson	No Laughing Matter, 1967
Iris Murdoch	The Black Prince, 1973
William Golding	Rites of Passage, 1980
Anthony Burgess (b.1917)	Earthly Powers, 1980

J. D. Salinger (b.1919), Catcher in the Rye, 1951 (Am.)

Suggestions for further reading

ABRAMS, M. H.: *A Glossary of Literary Terms*, 4th edn., Holt, Rinehart and Wiston, New York, 1981.

ALLEN, WALTER: *The English Novel*, Penguin Books, Harmondsworth, 1958.

BOOTH, WAYNE C.: *The Rhetoric of Fiction*, University of Chicago Press, Chicago, 1961.

FORSTER, E. M.: *Aspects of the Novel*, Edward Arnold, London, 1927.

HARVEY, SIR PAUL (ED.): *The Oxford Companion to English Literature*, 4th edn. revised by Dorothy Eagle, Clarendon Press, Oxford, 1967.

ISER, WOLFGANG: *The Act of Reading*, Routledge and Kegan Paul, London, 1966.

MILLIGAN, IAN: *The Novel in English: an Introduction*, Macmillan, London, 1983.

RABAN, JONATHAN: *The Technique of Modern Fiction*, Edward Arnold, London, 1967.

SCHOLES, ROBERT and KELLOG, ROBERT: *The Nature of Narrative*, Oxford University Press, London, 1966.

SEYMOUR-SMITH, MARTIN (ED.): *Novels and Novelists: a guide to the world of fiction*, Windward, London, 1980.

STEVENSON, LIONEL: *The English Novel: a panorama*, Constable, London, 1960.

WELLEK, R. and WARREN, A.: *Theory of Literature*, Penguin Books, Harmondsworth, 1963.

Index

SUBJECTS

anti-novel, 47–51
autobiographical novel, 58, 66
character, imaginative appeal of fictional characters, 9–10; literary and psychological meanings compared, 102; 'round' and 'flat', 103; the 'type', 45, 102
design, see plot
drama, and the technique of fiction, 32–6
epic, and the novel, 15, 42–3
epistolary novel, 14, 29–34
history, the novel as, 36–46
irony, 99, 112–13
metaphor, its use in the novel, 99
narrative voice, 50, 108–13
narrator, function, of, 45, 49, 96–7; types of, 101
novel in letters, see epistolary novel
picaresque novel, 14, 20–8
plot, 97–101; of *Washington Square*, 107–9
point of view, in the novel, 101
reader, the 'implied' (or 'fictitious'), 16, 103
reading, how we read a novel, 7–11,

15–17, 94; a formal approach, 16–17; the historical approach, 17; a thematic approach, 15
romance, distinguished from the novel, 13
scene, 36, 98, 107
setting, 103–4
'showing', distinguished from 'telling', 98, 107
story, distinguished from the novel, 90, 95–6, 112
'stream of consciousness', 91
structure, see plot
summary, its use by the novelist, 98, 107
surrealism, and the novel, 51
symbolism, and the novel, 100
theme(s), of the novel: adventure, 92–3; family, 84; the hero in the making, 53–67; inner worlds, 89–91; love and marriage, 81–4; politics, 88–9; the social novel, 81–4, 85–8; Utopia/Dystopia, 89; women in the novel, 67–81
truth, and fiction in the novel, 8–9, 13, 37–9, 40, 43

AUTHORS AND WORKS PRINCIPALLY DISCUSSED

Austen, Jane: *Emma*, 34–6, 68–71, 95; *Pride and Prejudice*, 67–8, 84, 99
Brontë, Charlotte: *Jane Eyre*, 71–3; *Villette*, 73–5
Brontë, Emily: *Wuthering Heights*, 71–2
Cervantes (Saavedra), Miguel de: *Don Quixote*, 11, 12, 13, 36–9

Conrad, Joseph: *Nostromo*, 87; *The Secret Agent*, 92
Defoe, Daniel: *Colonel Jack*, 39–41; *Moll Flanders*, 13–14; *Robinson Crusoe*, 29
Dickens, Charles: *Bleak House*, 84, 85–6; *David Copperfield*, 24, 58, 59–62, 66; *Great Expectations*, 62; *Hard Times*, 88, 95–6; *Little*

124 · Index

Further titles

ENGLISH POETRY
CLIVE T. PROBYN

The first aim of this Handbook is to describe and explain the technical aspects of poetry – all those daunting features in poetry's armoury from metre, form and theme to the iamb, caesura, ictus and heptameter. The second aim is to show how these features have earned their place in the making of poetry and the way in which different eras have applied fresh techniques to achieve the effect desired. Thus the effectiveness of poetic expression is shown to be closely linked to the appropriateness of the technique employed, and in this way the author hopes the reader will gain not only a better understanding of the value of poetic technique, but also a better 'feel' for poetry as a whole.

Clive T. Probyn is Professor of English at Monash University, Victoria, Australia.

A DICTIONARY OF LITERARY TERMS
MARTIN GRAY

Over one thousand literary terms are dealt with in this Handbook, with definitions, explanations and examples. Entries range from general topics (comedy, epic, metre, romanticism) to more specific terms (acrostic, enjambment, malapropism, onomatopoeia) and specialist technical language (catalexis, deconstruction, *haiku*, paeon). In other words, this single, concise volume should meet the needs of anyone searching for clarification of terms found in the study of literature.

Martin Gray is Lecturer in English at the University of Stirling.

AN INTRODUCTION TO LITERARY CRITICISM
RICHARD DUTTON

This is an introduction to a subject that has received increasing emphasis in the study of literature in recent years. As a means of identifying the underlying principles of the subject, the author examines the way in which successive eras and individual critics have applied different yardsticks by which to judge literary output. In this way the complexities of modern criticism are set in the perspective of its antecedents, and seen as only the most recent links in a chain of changing outlooks and methods of approach. The threads of this analysis are drawn together in the concluding chapter, which offers a blueprint for the practice of criticism.

Richard Dutton is Lecturer in English Literature at the University of Lancaster.

The first 200 titles

The author of this Handbook

IAN MILLIGAN was educated at the University of Glasgow where he gained the degrees of MA and MED. After teaching in the Royal High School, Edinburgh, he became a lecturer in English at Moray House College of Education, Edinburgh. He now lectures in the Department of English Studies at the University of Stirling. He has published articles on education, on the teaching of literature and on nineteenth- and twentieth-century literature. He is the author of York Notes on Jane Austen's *Northanger Abbey*, Richard Hughes's *A High Wind in Jamaica* and L. P. Hartley's *The Shrimp and the Anemone*.